HIKER'S GUIDE
To the Mount Zirkel
Wilderness Area

HIKER'S GUIDE

to the Mount Zirkel
WILDERNESS AREA

Jay and Therese Thompson

PRUETT PUBLISHING COMPANY
BOULDER, COLORADO

Printed in the United States
10 9 8 7 6 5 4 3 2 1

Library of Congress Cataloging-in-Publication Data

Thompson, Jay, 1960–
    Hiker's guide to the Mount Zirkel Wilderness area : with additional trails in the Routt National Forest / Jay and Therese Thompson.
        p.   cm.
    Includes index.
    ISBN 0-87108-815-0 : $13.95
    1. Hiking—Colorado—Mount Zirkel Wilderness—Guidebooks. 2. Hiking—Colorado—Routt National Forest—Guidebooks. 3. Mount Zirkel Wilderness (Colo.)—Guidebooks. 4. Routt National Forest (Colo.)—Guidebooks. I. Thompson, Therese, 1965–   . II. Title.
GV199.42.C62M688   1992
917.88´14—dc20   92-1210
                                                                            CIP

Cover and book design by Cover to Cover Design, Denver, Colorado
Photographs by Jay and Therese Thompson

Contents

Destinations in the Western Mount Zirkel Wilderness:

Destinations in the Eastern Mount Zirkel Wilderness:

Destinations in the Central Mount Zirkel Wilderness:

Destinations in the Surrounding Routt National Forest:

Introduction

With a high point just over 12,000 feet, the Mount Zirkel Wilderness is often overlooked in favor of the 14,000-foot peaks that have made Colorado hiking famous. Although lacking the renown of Colorado's tallest mountains, the Mount Zirkel Wilderness offers a spectacular array of peaks, valleys, lakes, and streams that collectively create a hiker's paradise.

The Mount Zirkel Wilderness was one of five Colorado wilderness areas created by the Wilderness Act of 1964. The Wilderness Act decreed that wilderness is a place "where the earth and its community of life are untrammeled by man, where man himself is a visitor who does not remain." The act further defined wilderness as an area that provides "outstanding opportunities for solitude or a primitive and unconfined type of recreation." In an effort to preserve their austere character, wilderness areas are closed to any form of mechanized travel (including mountain bikes) and can be explored only by trail. Colorado now has twenty-five designated Wilderness Areas that cover 2.7 million acres, or about four percent of the land area. State wilderness legislation in 1980 added broad expanses of land south of Mount Zirkel, and the Mount Zirkel Wilderness currently encompasses nearly 140,000 acres of the Park Range south of the Wyoming border in north-central Colorado. Pending wilderness legislation proposes adding up to 36,000 additional acres to the northern portion of the Wilderness Area.

The Wilderness Area takes its name from Mount Zirkel, which, at 12,180 feet, serves as the centerpiece of and highest point within the Wilderness. Clarence King, who led the Fortieth Parallel Survey of this area in 1874, named Mount Zirkel in honor of Ferdinand Zirkel, a German petrologist who accompanied King on the survey.

This guidebook describes hikes throughout the Wilderness. We have attempted to cover all the major destinations and trails, but the immenseness of the area necessitates that a few be omitted. The book is divided into four sections. Three sections feature hikes in each of the three different regions of the Wilderness. The final section highlights day hikes to easily accessible destinations just outside the Wilderness boundary in the surrounding Routt National Forest.

The hikes described range from short, easy walks to multiday backpacking excursions. We have tried to include numerous hikes at each level of difficulty. This guide focuses on hikes that do not

1

require technical gear (crampons, snowshoes), which limits the accessibility of most destinations to the period from July 1 to October 1 in most years. These dates are averages and will vary with the destination elevation and depth of snowpack from the preceding winter. We prefer hiking in September, when the trails are nearly deserted, the air crisp, the fish seem a wee bit more cooperative, and the fiery gold aspens futher enhance the already spectacular vistas.

Many of the hikes can be done in a half or full day with only a small daypack for gear. Arriving at the trailhead the night before longer day hikes will provide you with plenty of time to reach your destination and still maintain a leisurely pace. Several National Forest Service campgrounds skirt the edges of the wilderness and can serve as "base camps" for day hikes.

Our purpose in writing this book is not to encourage throngs of hikers to descend upon the fragile Mount Zirkel Wilderness. Sadly, signs of overuse and misuse are already visible in some parts of the Wilderness. Instead, we hope to help those who choose to visit this magical place to fully enjoy and appreciate the wonders it has to offer. We encourage hikers using this guidebook to leave no trace of their visit. Every person can make a difference. Increased use does not necessarily lead to abuse if educated and caring visitors treat the land with respect.

Always review the Wilderness regulations before beginning your hike.

Backcountry Ethics

The Mount Zirkel Wilderness is a beautiful place to visit. We can ensure it retains its natural beauty for years if all human visitors treat the wilderness with respect and follow a few simple back-country practices.

The principles of "low-impact camping" keep wild areas natural. The visitor's goal in low-impact camping is to leave trails and camp-sites exactly as he or she found them (or better) with no human trace. Some rules to follow:

1. Read the Wilderness regulations at the trailhead each time you hike in the Mount Zirkel Wilderness. Even if you have read them before, check to see if the regulations have changed. Some of the most popular lakes currently have camping restrictions (no camping within a quarter-mile of the lake) in order to allow overused areas to revegetate. These restrictions may change in the future.

2. Stay on trails at all times. Do not take shortcuts, especially across switchbacks, meadows, or tundra. When too many hikers take shortcuts, fragile plant life is damaged and the trampled area loses its vegetation. Deeply rutted shortcuts may also cause damage to the trail itself because of resulting high water runoff. The only time of year when an exception can be made to this rule is in early summer, when snowmelt runoff floods trails, especially those through meadows. If the trail you are following turns into a rapidly running stream, walk alongside it.

    3. "Pack it in, pack it out." Pack out all litter, extra food, and camping equipment you bring into the wilderness. Do not try to burn litter such as aluminum and metal cans in campfires—they do not burn completely. Do not leave cigarette butts, gum wrappers, or trash of any kind on the trail.

    4. Do not build a campfire unless absolutely necessary (for heat or cooking in an emergency). Campfires scar the ground and may adversely affect the wilderness experience of the next camper. Collecting dead wood for campsites can, over time, deplete an area of downed wood. Do not cut green vegetation of any sort. We pack in a lightweight backpacking stove and avoid campfires altogether.

    5. Never wash yourself or your dishes directly in a lake or stream. Take water you intend to use for washing away from the lake or stream and use biodegradable soap. Rinse off by pouring pans or water bottles full of water over your body (or dishes). Bio-degradable soap for camping can be found in most camping/backpacking specialty stores.

    6. Practice good sanitary hygiene. Minimize the use of toilet paper and bury feces at least two hundred feet from any trail, stream, or lake. Cover feces with at least six inches of soil to aid in decomposition. If you hike with a dog, try to keep it from leaving droppings within two hundred feet of any source of water.

Fishing

    The Mount Zirkel Wilderness offers excellent backcountry fishing opportunities. The thrill of catching brightly colored trout at a remote mountain lake is the highlight of many hiking adventures. In order to help plan your choice of destination, we have included general information about angling opportunities along routes or at final destinations. Before casting into these wilderness waters, remember that the high elevation of the Mount Zirkel Wilderness results in a short growing season for fish because most lakes are ice-covered for seven to eight months of the year. Under such extreme conditions fish grow slowly and may require several years to reach catchable size. We encourage all anglers to practice catch-and-release fishing whenever possible. However, adding one or two fresh trout to a backcountry dinner is a special pleasure, and this type of sensible consumption will not harm fish populations. Fishing success in high-country lakes is very unpredictable. At one lake, we each caught a fish on the first five casts, only to go the next two hours without a single nibble. Regardless of how many fish are ultimately caught (and carefully released), the experience of fishing these high mountain gems is truly rewarding.

Safety

We do not want to make hiking in the Mount Zirkel Wilderness, or any part of Colorado, sound dangerous or only for the experienced hiker. Anyone and everyone can hike, camp, and thoroughly enjoy the Rocky Mountains. In many years of hiking in Colorado, neither of us has ever had an injury more severe than sunburn or experienced weather harsh enough to endanger our lives. However, it is best to be prepared for the worst, just in case. Be sure to tell somebody where you are going and when you plan to return. Avoid hiking alone, unless you are an experienced hiker who is familiar with the area and safety/emergency-survival techniques. Nothing can replace common sense when hiking or camping in the backcountry. The rest of this chapter contains general information on weather and safety for hikers of all experience levels.

Weather

Weather in the Mount Zirkel Wilderness can change quickly and unexpectedly. A classic example of the fickle nature of weather there involved a September trip we made to Gilpin Lake. We ate dinner in the sun with a light breeze blowing. Within thirty minutes we were in our tent taking refuge from the most ferocious thunderstorm we had ever seen. In this case we could hear the wind and thunder moving up the valley toward us twenty minutes before it began to rain, but many times hikers have little or no advance notice of approaching inclement weather.

Afternoon thunderstorms are common in the Rockies, especially from late June to early September. Storms can be severe and bring rain, snow, or hail during any month of the hiking season. Temperatures can plummet thirty to forty degrees in a couple of hours. Be prepared with rain gear and warm clothes in case of unexpected storms.

Lightning. Although rain or snow can make for an uncomfortable hike, lightning is one of the biggest threats to a hiker's safety. If you are hiking along a high point or barren ridge and can see or hear a storm in the distance, retreat as quickly as possible to lower ground. Hair standing on end on your arms, legs, or head (static electricity) is a warning sign of an imminent lightning strike. If you do not have time to get to lower ground, *do not* take shelter under prominent landscape features like high trees. Remember that a *direct* lighting hit is *not necessary* in order for a strike to be fatal.

Sun. Some of the most severe sunburns we have experienced occurred while we were hiking at high elevations on cool but sunny days. Remember, even though it feels chilly and may be overcast, you are more susceptible to sunburn at higher elevations. A good rule of thumb is to keep as much of your body covered as is comfortable and wear a hat to shade your face. Do not sleep, or allow children to sleep, in direct sunlight. It is good practice to always wear sunscreen when hiking.

Darkness. Even if you are planning only a day hike, someone in your party may get lost or injured; always be prepared to spend an unexpected night in the wilderness. Bring matches in a waterproof container, flashlights (one per hiker), and warm clothes. Once you realize you will not make it back to the trailhead before dark, find a sheltered rock or tree and get your group as comfortable as possible before it is completely dark. It is not a good idea to try and hike and/or move around more than necessary after dark because of the danger of getting lost or twisting an ankle.

Illness

Heat Exhaustion. While usually more common in warmer latitudes, heat exhaustion can occur while hiking in Colorado's mountains. Warm, sunny days combined with strenuous hikes through open country take a toll on even the most experienced hiker. Combine these factors with insufficient water and salt intake and you are a candidate for heat exhaustion. To avoid becoming a victim, snack on salty foods and drink plenty of water at regular intervals while you hike, whether or not you feel thirsty.

Altitude Sickness. Although generally not a problem at altitudes commonly encountered in the Mount Zirkel Wilderness, some individuals suffer the symptoms of altitude sickness at elevations as low as 8,000 feet. These symptoms range from minor (headache, nausea, loss of appetite) to severe (dizziness, loss of judgment, retinal bleeding). The treatment for all cases of altitude sickness is to get the victim to a lower altitude as quickly as possible.

Hypothermia. Hypothermia occurs when the core body temperature falls below normal. Wet clothes combined with a cloudy day, cold weather, or wind can bring on this condition quickly, even during summer months. The first phase is exposure and exhaustion—if you begin to shiver or lose control of your hands, hypothermia is occurring. Fellow hikers must furnish heat immediately, because the afflicted person will soon become disoriented and unaware of his or her deteriorating condition. If someone in your group becomes hypothermic: 1. get the victim out of the rain and wind; 2. light a fire if possible; 3. strip off the victim's wet clothes. In less-severe cases, warm dry clothing for the victim will correct the problem; in severe cases where the victim is disoriented, put him or her in a sleeping bag with another person (both stripped)—the skin-to-skin body-heat transfer should bring the victim's body temperature back up to normal.

Giardia. Giardia is a waterborne parasite that can be a serious threat to your health. The cyst stage of the Giardia protozoan is spread by droppings from dogs, horses, cattle, deer, beavers, and even humans. Giardia is most commonly associated with beaver ponds—do not take drinking water from these areas or any area of stagnant water. Ingesting the parasite can lead to giardiasis, with symptoms appearing anywhere from several days to several weeks later. Symptoms are commonly characterized by severe diarrhea, weight loss, fatigue, and cramps. Ingesting Giardia can be avoided by using water-filter devices when taking drinking water from streams, using iodine crystals, or boiling water for several minutes. If you suspect you may have giardiasis, consult your doctor immediately.

Wild Animals

Do not harass, or allow dogs to harass, wildlife you encounter while hiking or camping. Do not feed or attempt to pet wild animals—they will bite! If wild animals become accustomed to being fed by humans they will eventually rely on human help to survive, concentrate in areas where humans frequent, and struggle to survive through the winter when humans are scarce.

Animals that wander into your camp will smell food and search for it—you want to be certain they cannot get to it and that the smell does not lead them to your tent. To keep wild animals away from your tent at night, do not bring food or clothes that smell like food into your tent. We avoid bringing foodlike items, such as toothpaste, into our tent as well. Although few animals would harm you to get the food in your tent, some have been known to chew holes in tents or clothing to get to food. There are no grizzly bears in the Mount Zirkel Wilderness, but black bears and other animals will get into food left on the ground. It is a good practice to set up a separate cooking area well away from your tent. We always hang our food bag at least two hundred feet from our camp, suspended at least ten feet off the ground, and out at least four feet from the tree trunk.

Signs

A word of caution about signs in the Mount Zirkel Wilderness. In general, signs at most trailheads and trail junctions point you in the proper direction. Unfortunately, there are exceptions to this rule; signs may be present one day and gone the next. Do not depend on them to direct you to your destination. At best, signs should serve to confirm what you already expect based on your map and the hike description. If you discover a missing or damaged sign, report it to the Routt National Forest office so it can be replaced.

Some of the trails described in this book are seldom traveled and rarely maintained. As a result, they become overgrown and difficult to follow. Faint sections of trails are often marked by a small pile of rocks, known as a *cairn,* alongside the appropriate route. Whenever a trail fades or disappears, look carefully for a nearby cairn to lead you in the proper direction.

Season

Trail openings vary from year to year depending on the elevation of the trail, amount of snowfall the previous winter, and scheduling of forest service trail-repair crews. It is always a good idea to call the ranger's office before you leave home and ask for information on trail conditions and accessibility. In a year with average snowfall, some of the lower-elevation trails/destinations can be reached by late June if you do not mind getting your feet wet in swampy meadows and on slushy trails. In most years, all trails will be accessible by mid-July. Generally, the latest time of year you can hike in the Mount Zirkel Wilderness will be mid-October. Late-season hiking requires extra precautions to account for potentially severe weather and the presence of hunters. Wearing a bright orange ("hunter orange") cap and vest is essential during fall hunting seasons. We each carry an extra sweater, hat, and pair of gloves in our daypacks for our autumn excursions.

Format for the Hike Descriptions

The following information is provided at the beginning of each hike description.

1. Name of hike. All hikes are named for their final destination(s). Be careful not to become too "destination-oriented"; a walk in the Wilderness does not have to end at a spot that is named on the map. If you get a late start or just are not feeling energetic, do not push yourself too hard simply for the sake of saying "I made it."

2. Trailhead. The name given here is usually taken from one of two sources: the name of the trailhead itself (e.g., Diamond Park trailhead, Base Camp trailhead), which may be unrelated to the trails that depart from that trailhead; or the name of the ultimate destination reached from that trailhead (e.g., Rainbow Lakes trailhead).

Trails in the Mount Zirkel Wilderness have both a name and a number (e.g., Rainbow Lakes Trail #1130). In this book we have included both trail names and numbers. Once you have selected a hike, take a few minutes to read through the directions to the trailhead with a map in front of you. This will give you a good idea of where you are headed before you set out.

3. Starting/ending elevation. These are the elevations at the trailhead and at the final destination. Pay close attention to these numbers, because they will help you gauge the difficulty of a particular hike. In most cases, the ending elevation is also the highest elevation; most hikes start from a low elevation and climb to a higher one.

When you plan a hike early (late June through mid-July) or late (after mid-September) in the season, look carefully at the ending elevation. High-elevation sites (any of the mountain summits or high-altitude lakes) will be inaccessible into early summer and become inaccessible earlier in the fall. We are consistently amazed by the tenacity of snow in the Colorado high country—snow can persist in the Mount Zirkel Wilderness virtually year-round.

4. Distance. This is the *round-trip* distance in miles from trailhead to final destination.

5. Time required. This is the estimated time to complete the *round-trip* hike based on distance and elevation change. Times are based on a pace of about two miles per hour, adjusted for uphill or downhill walking.

Trails above 10,000 feet can remain snow-covered well into July.

6. Rating. This rating is based mainly on elevation gained during the hike. A long (eight-mile), fairly level hike will be rated easy, while a short, steep (three miles with 1,500 feet of elevation gain) hike will be rated moderate.

7. Maps. These are U.S. Geological Survey (USGS) topographic maps that cover the area from the trailhead to the final destination. We also recommend the Routt National Forest map because it includes road and trail numbers. Hikers should carry USGS maps when hiking and should not depend solely on the forest service map. Do not rely on the maps provided in this book—they are limited to the area immediately surrounding the trail and are intended as general guides only. The maps in this book include large letters that correspond to readily identifiable features or important junctions you will encounter during the hike; each hike description refers to these letters. Use the letters to check your progress as you hike.

Another option is to use maps produced by the Trails Illustrated Company. Each of their maps takes the place of eight topographic maps and is printed on waterproof, tearproof plastic. We found these maps to be virtually indestructible. Trails Illustrated maps include both the trail name and number and show some new trails that have been added since the topographic maps were last revised. Unless you are planning to travel off-trail with map and compass, the Trails Illustrated maps will serve most of your hiking needs. The two Trails Illustrated maps that cover the Mount Zirkel Wilderness are Steamboat Springs North (#117) and Hahn's Peak (#116). Steamboat Springs South (#118) covers the Routt National Forest south of the Wilderness. Trails Illustrated maps can be purchased at most camping/backpacking specialty stores.

8. Main Attractions. Each hike in this book is unique. We have included a sentence or two about what we feel is most notable about a particular hike or destination.

Equipment List

Day Hike

Comfortable, lightweight daypack
Plenty of water, or a water-filter system, or iodine crystals
Food for snacking while you hike
Enough food for one extra day, in case of emergency
Trail guide and topographic maps
Compass
Warm clothes: extra sweatshirt, sweatpants, wool socks, gloves
Rain gear
Sunscreen, sunglasses
First aid kit (moleskin for blisters, Band-Aids, aspirin, one roll of
    three-inch gauze)
Insect repellent
Toilet paper (in a plastic bag to keep it dry)
Pocket knife/army knife
Flashlight (one per hiker)
Matches in a waterproof container
Camera
Fishing gear, license, regulations
Animal, plant, or other appropriate field guides
Binoculars

Additional Items for a Longer Trip

Extra pair of hiking boots or shoes
Food for as many days as you plan to be camping, plus one extra day
Warm clothes (same as above plus long underwear, warm hat)
Lightweight tent
Waterproof ground cloth to put under tent
Sleeping bags and pads
Backpacking stove and extra fuel
Rope or nylon cord and waterproof sack to hang food
Two bags to carry trash out
Plastic garbage bag to pull over backpack at night
Cooking and eating utensils, spices in small containers
Can opener (small army type)
Biodegradable dishwashing soap
Cigarette lighter (in case matches get wet)
Trowel for digging "bathroom" holes

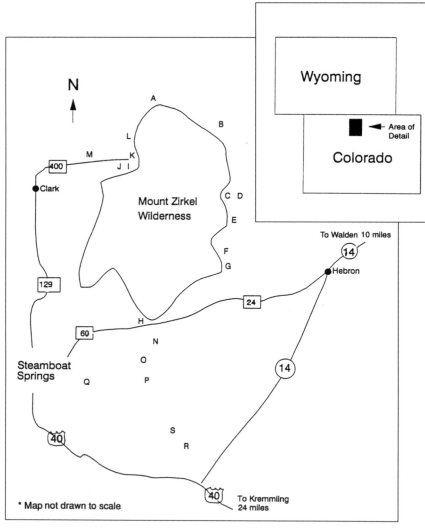

Key to Trailheads

A. West Fork
B. Big Creek
C. Lake Katherine
D. Grizzly-Helena (on Lone Pine Rd.)
E. Rainbow Lakes
F. Grizzly-Helena (to Agua Fria Lake)
G. Newcomb Creek
H. Wyoming Trail (at Buffalo Pass)
I. North Lake
J. Three Island Lake

K. Slavonia
L. Diamond Park
M. Hinman Lake
N. Grizzly Lake
O. Lake Dinosaur
P. Long Lake
Q. Fish Creek Falls
R. Rabbit Ears
S. Base Camp

Destinations in the Western
Mount Zirkel Wilderness

The western portion of the Mount Zirkel Wilderness features some of the most popular hikes within the Wilderness Area. The Slavonia trailhead is the busiest access point of the entire Wilderness, often drawing over one hundred hikers on summer weekends. Its popularity is well deserved, because the area features several reasonably easy walks to beautiful mountain lakes. The highest point in the Wilderness, Mount Zirkel, is also best approached from the western boundary.

The popularity of Gilpin Lake, Three Island Lake, and Gold Creek Lake is offset by the relative obscurity of other destinations in the western Wilderness. Dome Lake, Lake Diana, Gem Lake, and the Wolverine Basin lakes involve longer hikes and thus are rarely visited. Also included in this section is the hike to Slavonia Mining Camp, the most complete historical site in the Mount Zirkel Wilderness.

Directions to the various trailheads in this section are given from Steamboat Springs, which is the largest town on the western side of the Wilderness.

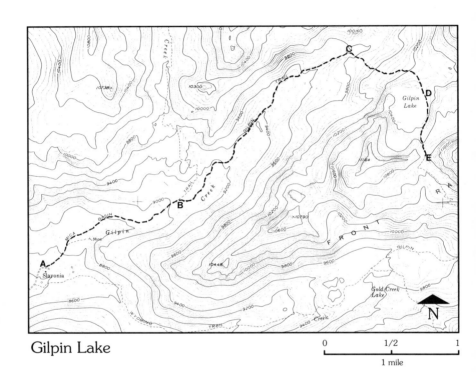

Gilpin Lake

Gilpin Lake

Trailhead
> *Slavonia/Gilpin Lake Trail (#1161)*

Starting elevation
> *8,460 feet*

Ending elevation
> *10,338 feet*

Distance (round trip)
> *8 miles*

Time required (round trip)
> *4 hours*

Rating
> *Easy/Moderate*

Maps
> *7.5' Mount Zirkel*
> *Routt National Forest*

Main attractions
> *Impressive views of Sawtooth Range; deep, blue alpine lake; can be combined with other hikes to create loop hikes of one to several days.*

With its deep blue waters and spectacular setting, Gilpin Lake is deservedly one of the most popular destinations in the Mount Zirkel Wilderness. Unfortunately, overuse and misuse have led to the closure of Gilpin Lake to camping within a quarter-mile of its shore. Be sure to read the Wilderness regulations carefully if you are planning to backpack in this region.

To reach the trailhead, take Routt County 129 north from Steamboat Springs for 17.4 miles to Forest Service Road 400 (Seedhouse Road). Follow Forest Service Road 400 for 11.9 miles until it dead-ends at the Slavonia trailhead. The road to the trailhead is an all-weather dirt road that does not require four-wheel-drive.

From the Slavonia trailhead (**Point A**), follow the trail several hundred yards to a fork; take the left fork toward Gilpin Lake (the right fork leads to Gold Creek Lake and beyond). The trail winds through stands of aspen before entering the Mount Zirkel Wilderness

Rewarding view of Gilpin Lake from the ridge above its southeastern shore. Big Agnes Mountain is visible in the background.

about ¾-mile from the trailhead. About ¼-mile after entering the Wilderness, the trail forks again (**Point B**). Stay to the right and follow the trail as it heads away from Gilpin Creek and crosses Mica Creek. Slowly gain elevation through the forested valley before dropping alongside, but not crossing, Gilpin Creek. This trail receives heavy use and is thus well defined, but the rocky terrain is still rough in spots.

About 2.5 miles from the trailhead, the trail enters an open area with small trees and willows. A long ridgeline can be seen directly ahead. The highest point on the ridge is an unnamed peak (elevation 12,006 feet) often mistaken for nearby Mount Zirkel, which is out of view to the north. Cross Gilpin Creek (**Point C**) near the upper end of the meadow and enter the trees. If camping within ¼-mile of Gilpin Lake is still prohibited, there are many good camping spots on both sides of the creek and in the trees after crossing Gilpin Creek. If you plan to camp, be aware that the trail leading to and beyond Gilpin Lake is quite steep; we recommend setting up camp near Gilpin Creek before continuing to the lake. After crossing Gilpin Creek, the trail gains 500 feet in the final ¾-mile to Gilpin Lake (**Point D**).

The deep, blue-green waters of Gilpin Lake (10,338 feet, 29 acres) are nestled in spectacularly rugged country. This is one of the most picturesque destinations in the Wilderness Area. Fishing can be quite good for plump brook trout, especially along the rocky shore opposite the main trail. If Gilpin Lake is as far as you plan to go, take time to follow the trail along the east shore and up the switchbacks at the south end of the lake. The panoramic view of the lake and Big and Little Agnes mountains from the ridge (**Point E**) is worth the effort.

Beyond Gilpin Lake, the trail drops steeply down from the ridge above the lake before intersecting the trail to Red Dirt Pass and Ute Pass, about 1 mile past the lake. The trail continues west to Gold Creek Lake before returning to the Slavonia trailhead. The hikes to Gilpin and Gold Creek lakes can be combined to form a 9-mile loop featuring beautiful alpine scenery and virtually no backtracking.

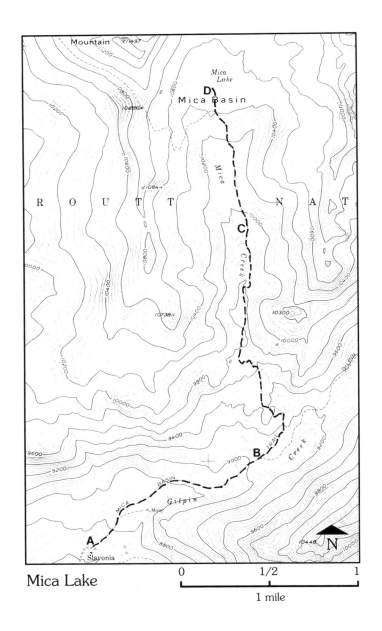

Mica Lake

0   1/2   1

1 mile

Mica Lake

Trailhead
> *Slavonia/Gilpin Lake Trail (#1161 to #1162)*

Starting elevation
> *8,460 feet*

Ending elevation
> *10,428 feet*

Distance (round trip)
> *8 miles*

Time required (round trip)
> *4 hours*

Rating
> *Easy/Moderate*

Maps
> *7.5' Mount Zirkel*
> *Routt National Forest*

Main attractions
> *Short day hike to a scenic lake; close to Seedhouse Camp-round; least-crowded destination from a busy trailhead.*

The walk to Mica Basin and Mica Lake is a leisurely half-day hike featuring beautiful views, fishing, and an escape from the crowds. The Slavonia/Gilpin Lake trailhead is a popular access point into the Mount Zirkel Wilderness, but most hikers journey to Gilpin Lake or Gold Creek Lake and bypass the spur trail to Mica Lake.

To reach the trailhead, take Routt County 129 north from Steamboat Springs for 17.4 miles to Forest Service Road 400 (Seedhouse Road). Follow Forest Service Road 400 for 11.9 miles until it dead-ends at the Slavonia trailhead. The road to the trailhead is an all-weather dirt road that does not require four-wheel-drive.

From the Slavonia trailhead (**Point A**), follow the trail several hundred yards to a fork; take the left fork toward Gilpin and Mica lakes (the right fork leads to Gold Creek Lake and beyond). Gradually gain elevation as you climb through a large grove of aspen. About ¾-mile from the trailhead, a sign marks the Wilderness

Mica Lake.

boundary. It is about ¼-mile to the Mica Lake Trail turnoff from the Wilderness boundary. The trail to Mica Lake (**Point B**) heads off to the left (north) just opposite a large dome-shaped rock on the right side of the Gilpin Lake Trail. On our last visit, the Mica Lake Trail (#1162) was not marked by a sign, as it had been previously, but the trail is distinct and marked by a rock cairn and signpost.

After leaving the Gilpin Lake Trail, the trail to Mica Lake switchbacks through numerous large boulders and rock outcrops. After 1.5 miles, enter a large meadow (**Point C**) and catch a glimpse of the rocky crags that surround Mica Lake and form Mica Basin. The view from this meadow gives the impression that Mica Lake is just over the next knoll, but there is still some ground to cover. After passing through several smaller meadows and continuing to steadily gain altitude, the trail arrives at Mica Lake (**Point D**) 2.5 miles and 1,400 feet above the Gilpin Lake Trail.

Mica Lake (10,428 feet, 6 acres) is nestled under the steep-sided slopes of Mica Basin. The lake contains brook and rainbow trout, but the fishing is only fair. Although this route is typically a day hike, there are backcountry campsites near the lake.

The Mica Lake Trail continues 5 miles northwest beyond the lake to its northern terminus at the Diamond Park trailhead.

Mount Zirkel

Trailhead
> Slavonia/Gilpin Lake Trail (#1161)

Starting elevation
> 8,460 feet

Ending elevation
> 12,180 feet

Distance (round trip)
> Loop hike via Gilpin Creek cutoff: 12 miles
> Via Gold Creek Lake and Red Dirt Pass: 15 miles

Time required (round trip)
> Loop hike via Gilpin Creek cutoff: 9 hours
> Via Gold Creek Lake and Red Dirt Pass: 9.5 hours

Rating
> Difficult

Maps
> 7.5′ Mount Zirkel
> Routt National Forest

Main attractions
> Highest point in the Mount Zirkel Wilderness; spectacular
> views from the summit.

Although often overlooked in the land of 14,000-foot peaks,
Mount Zirkel (12,180 feet) is as majestic as most of the taller and
more renowned Colorado mountains. For many, the hike to the
summit of Mount Zirkel is the highlight of their hiking adventures in
the Mount Zirkel Wilderness. From late July until September the
hike to the summit is nontechnical and requires only sturdy hiking
boots and stamina. Plan on getting an early start, because it is
advisable to be off the summit by noon to avoid the frequent
afternoon thunderstorms. Mount Zirkel can be approached from
either the east or west side of the Wilderness; the described routes
are from the west.

Two routes to the summit are described below. The first is a
considerably shorter loop hike that requires extensive off-trail travel.
It is described in detail and recommended for experienced hikers only.

23

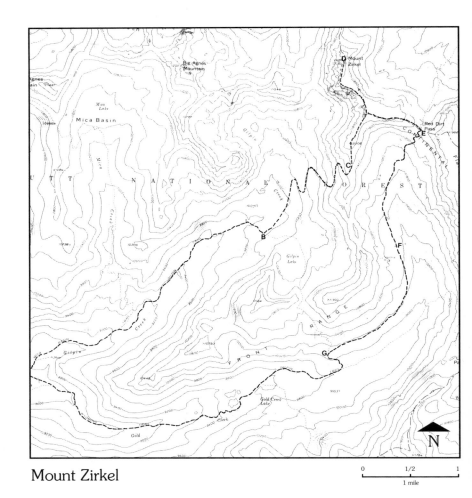

Mount Zirkel

0   1/2   1

1 mile

Unnamed peak (elevation 12,006 feet) from the Gilpin Lake Trail.

The second route is the longer, conventional, approach, which follows trails for all but the final mile. It is only briefly described here; further description is provided in the Slavonia Mining Camp hike narration on page 33.

To reach the trailhead, take Routt County 129 north from Steamboat Springs for 17.4 miles to Forest Service Road 400 (Seedhouse Road). Follow Forest Service Road 400 for 11.9 miles until it dead-ends at the Slavonia trailhead. The road to the trailhead is an all-weather dirt road that does not require four-wheel-drive.

Loop Hike via Gilpin Creek Cutoff to Mount Zirkel

From the Slavonia trailhead (**Point A**), follow the trail several hundred yards to a fork; take the left fork toward Gilpin Lake (the right fork leads to Gold Creek Lake and beyond). Wind through stands of aspen before entering the Mount Zirkel Wilderness ¾-mile from the trailhead. About ¼-mile after entering the Wilderness, the trail forks again. Stay to the right and follow the trail as it heads away from Gilpin Creek and crosses Mica Creek. After about 2.5 miles the trail enters a meadow and a long ridgeline can be seen

Mount Zirkel. A trail register can be found on the highest of the three summits, the one farthest to the right.

straight ahead. The highest point on the ridge is an unnamed peak (elevation 12,006 feet) often mistaken for nearby Mount Zirkel, which is out of view to the north. The shortest route to the summit of Mount Zirkel involves climbing up the steep grassy slope to the right (south) of the unnamed peak to reach the top of the ridge. After crossing Gilpin Creek, leave the trail (**Point B**) and head for the slope to the right (south) of the unnamed peak. There is no defined trail, so stay on the grassy areas where the footing is better. Take frequent rests as you slowly switchback up the slope toward the top of the ridge. Arrive at the top of the ridge just south of the 12,006-foot peak (**Point C**). After taking in the view of the appropriately named Flattop Mountain to the east, scale the unnamed peak and continue heading north toward Mount Zirkel. Although there is no maintained trail, the route just below the ridge on the right (east) side provides good footing.

The three-pronged summit of Mount Zirkel becomes visible as you continue north along the ridgeline. When you arrive at the base of Mount Zirkel, scramble over large angular rocks until you reach the first of the three summits. Once you reach the easternmost and highest summit (**Point D**), search under the rocks for the trail register and add your name to those kindred spirits who have been here before you. The views from the summit are impressive: Little and Big Agnes mountains and the Sawtooth Range to the northwest, Fryingpan Basin directly below to the north, Red Dirt Pass and Flattop Mountain to the southeast, and Ute Pass directly south.

To create a loop hike for the return to the trailhead, head southeast from the summit, descending to the aptly named Red Dirt Pass (**Point E**) and picking up the trail toward Gilpin Lake. The trail switchbacks down from the top of the pass, enters a meadow, and drops below treeline. One and a half miles below Red Dirt Pass, you will pass two old miners' cabins below the abandoned Upper Slavonia Mine (**Point F**). Several hundred yards east of the cabins along the bank of Gold Creek lie the remains of a compressor that was once powered by creek water. The compressor and cabins date from about 1910, when the mine was in operation. Below the cabins the trail follows the route of the original wagon road that once led to the mine.

About ¼-mile beyond the cabins, bypass the turnoff to Ute Pass. The trail intersects the Gilpin Lake Trail (#1161) (**Point G**), 1 mile beyond the Ute Pass turnoff. Both forks lead back to the Slavonia trailhead. The shortest route is via the left fork, which passes by Gold Creek Lake. The right fork of the Gilpin Lake Trail climbs steeply over the ridge to Gilpin Lake before dropping down to Gilpin Creek and returning to the Slavonia trailhead.

Gold Creek Lake Route to Mount Zirkel

A longer route to the summit of Mount Zirkel follows the trail from the Slavonia trailhead past Gold Creek Lake to Red Dirt Pass. From the pass, head northwest for 1 mile along the wide ridge to the top of Mount Zirkel. This route is 3 miles longer than the route described above. However, since it follows a trail for all but the final mile, it requires about the same amount of time as the shorter route.

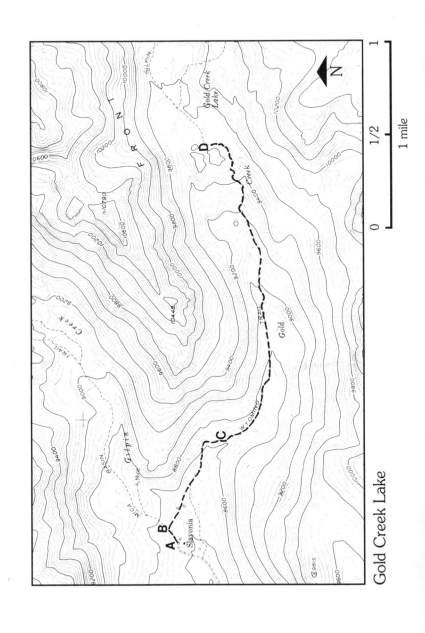

Gold Creek Lake

Gold Creek Lake

Trailhead
> *Slavonia/Gold Creek Lake Trail (#1127)*

Starting elevation
> *8,460 feet*

Ending elevation
> *9,555 feet*

Distance (round trip)
> *6.5 miles*

Time required (round trip)
> *3.5 hours*

Rating
> *Easy*

Maps
> *7.5' Mount Zirkel*
> *Routt National Forest*

Main attractions
> *Trail follows Gold Creek to lake; close to Seedhouse Campground; can be combined with other hikes to create loop hikes of one to several days.*

The trail to Gold Creek Lake offers a fairly short but beautiful hike into the Mount Zirkel Wilderness. The trail closely follows alongside Gold Creek up to the lake and, unlike other trails in the Wilderness, has bridges over all stream crossings. One of the most popular destinations in the Mount Zirkel Wilderness, Gold Creek Lake is lower in elevation than most of the other lakes and therefore is accessible earlier in the year. Because of its popularity and subsequent overuse, Gold Creek Lake is closed to camping and campfires within a quarter-mile of its shore. Be sure to read the Wilderness regulations posted at the trailhead carefully if you are planning to backpack in this part of the Wilderness.

To reach the trailhead, take Routt County 129 north from Steamboat Springs for 17.4 miles to Forest Service Road 400 (Seedhouse Road). Follow Forest Service Road 400 for 11.9 miles until it dead-ends at the Slavonia trailhead. The road to the

Gold Creek Lake from its northwest shore. The eastern part of the lake is hidden from view.

trailhead is an all-weather dirt road that does not require four-wheel-drive.

From the Slavonia trailhead (**Point A**), follow the trail several hundred yards to a point where it forks (**Point B**). Take the right fork toward Gold Creek Lake, Ute Pass, and Red Dirt Pass. The remains of an old building foundation can be seen just past the fork in the trail. The trail is well-defined and fairly level. Approximately ⅓-mile from the trailhead, hikers will notice the ruins of an old cabin alongside the trail. Just beyond this ruin a bridge crosses Gilpin Creek, and Gold Creek appears on the right. For the remainder of the hike the trail follows Gold Creek through spruce and fir forest with intermingled stands of aspen.

About 1 mile from the trailhead, climb up a ridge high above Gold Creek. At the peak of the ridge (**Point C**) stop and enjoy the spectacular views of Gold Creek far below. Fir, lodgepole pine, and spruce are all present atop this ridge. The trail winds another .25-mile before entering the Mount Zirkel Wilderness 1.25 miles from the trailhead. One and three-quarter miles from the trailhead the trail passes an impressive thirty-five-foot-high waterfall. A large, flat rock overlooking the waterfall provides an ideal platform for photographers. Two and three-quarter miles from the trailhead the trail steeply switchbacks away from Gold Creek. The trail returns to the creek again at mile 3 and remains level for the remaining ¼-mile until reaching Gold Creek Lake (**Point D**).

Gold Creek Lake (9,555 feet, 8 acres) is surrounded on the south, west, and east by spruce and fir. The north rim of the lake is dominated by a large rock outcropping. Good fishing spots for eight- to ten-inch brook trout can be found along the rock outcrop. If you are not continuing to Gilpin Lake, Red Dirt Pass, or Ute Pass, take time to walk the trail around Gold Creek Lake—the views to the north and east are worth the trip!

To continue to Gilpin Lake, Red Dirt Pass, or Ute Pass, pick up the trail just north of the rock outcropping on the north side of the lake. To make a scenic loop, follow the trail from Gold Creek Lake east about 1 mile to the turnoff to Gilpin Lake. Follow the Gilpin Lake Trail back to the trailhead for a memorable 9-mile loop through the Wilderness.

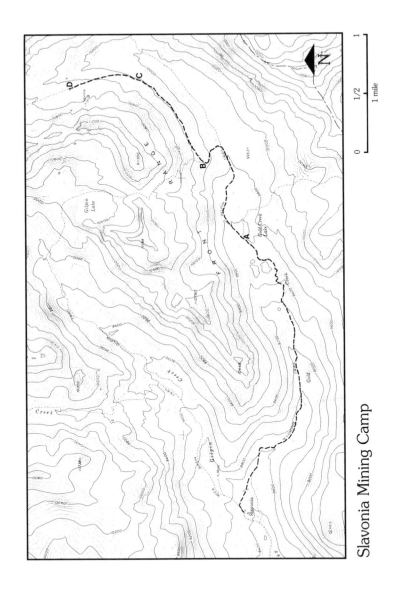

Slavonia Mining Camp

Slavonia Mining Camp

Trailhead
Slavonia/Gold Creek Lake Trail (#1127)
Starting elevation
8,460 feet
Ending elevation
10,000 feet
Distance (round trip)
11.5 miles
Time required (round trip)
6 hours
Rating
Moderate
Maps
7.5' Mount Zirkel
Routt National Forest
Main attractions
Opportunity to visit historic mining camp, cabins, and compressor ruins; only 2.5 miles beyond Gold Creek Lake.

Unlike many mountainous areas, the Mount Zirkel Wilderness is not rich in mining history. Although small, exploratory diggings can be found throughout the Wilderness, the Slavonia Mine is the area's best example of man's endless quest to strike it rich. The mine operated in the early 1900s, and the trail to the mine follows the road once used by wagons hauling miners and supplies to the site.

To reach the Slavonia mining camp, follow the hike narration for Gold Creek Lake (see page 29). The trail to the mining camp can be picked up on the north side of Gold Creek Lake, north of the large rock outcropping.

Shortly after leaving Gold Creek Lake, you will wind up among a jumble of large rocks and head downhill to a fork in the trail (**Point A**). The less-defined right fork leads to Lost Ranger Peak and Sheep Drive. The better-defined left fork leads to Ute Pass, Slavonia mining camp, Red Dirt Pass, and Gilpin Lake. Stay to the

Cabin ruins at the Slavonia mining camp. Red Dirt Pass is visible in the background.

left and almost immediately cross an unnamed creek that feeds into Gold Creek. One mile beyond Gold Creek Lake, drop alongside the creek and admire the impressive view straight ahead of the aptly named Flattop Mountain. The trail begins to wind steeply uphill away from the valley. At the Gilpin Lake turnoff (**Point B**), stay to the right and continue toward Red Dirt Pass. The trail stays up on the ridge above the valley beyond the Gilpin Lake turnoff, and Flattop Mountain still dominates the views to the east. About 2 miles beyond Gold Creek Lake a sign indicates an indistinct trail fork (**Point C**). The right fork leads to Ute Pass; stay to the left and continue toward Red Dirt Pass. One-quarter mile beyond the Ute Pass turnoff the remains of the Slavonia mining camp (**Point D**) come into view.

Along the main trail, two dilapidated cabins create a unique photo opportunity with Red Dirt Pass in the background. Those hikers with extra energy can find additional relics nearby. The remains of a hydraulically powered compressor lie alongside Gold Creek below the cabins. Closer inspection reveals that various parts of the compressor were patented in 1910 and 1911. On the hillside above the cabins is the old mine site. The main mine shaft reportedly

*Close-up of the old hydraulic compressor alongside Gold Creek
below the Slavonia mining camp.*

extended 350 feet into the west wall of Gold Creek Canyon, but is
now caved in (which is fortunate, because old mines should never
be entered). The rails that once carried ore carts are still present,
and one of the rusty carts lies below the abandoned mine.

Once you've finished exploring, you have the option of continuing to the summit of Mount Zirkel. If plenty of daylight remains
and the risk of thunderstorms is low, continue up the trail an
additional 1.5 miles to Red Dirt Pass. From the pass follow the
ridge northwest 1 mile to the summit of Mount Zirkel.

It is also possible to hike to the Slavonia Mine ruins via Gilpin
Lake. To hike from Gilpin Lake, follow the Gilpin Lake Trail
(#1161) over the ridge south of Gilpin Lake to its intersection with
the Gold Creek Lake Trail at Point B. Follow the directions, above,
from Point B to the ruins.

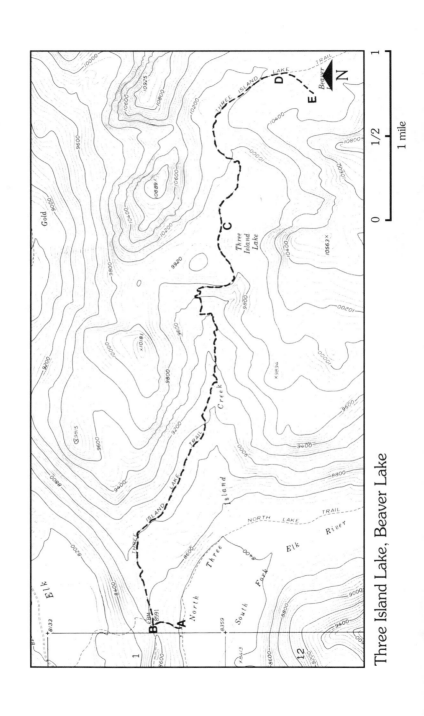

Three Island Lake, Beaver Lake

Three Island Lake, Beaver Lake

Trailhead

> *Three Island Lake Trailhead (#1163)*

Starting elevation

> *8,380 feet*

Ending elevation

> *Three Island Lake: 9,878 feet*
> *Beaver Lake: 10,340 feet*

Distance (round trip)

> *Three Island Lake: 7 miles*
> *Beaver Lake: 9.5 miles*

Time required (round trip)

> *Three Island Lake: 3.5 hours*
> *Beaver Lake: 4.5 hours*

Ratings

> *Three Island Lake: Easy*
> *Beaver Lake: Easy/Moderate*

Maps

> *7.5' Mount Zirkel*
> *Routt National Forest*

Main attractions

> *Short hike to a large lake; good fishing for brook trout; solitude.*

Three Island Lake is one of the most popular destinations in the Mount Zirkel Wilderness, offering a combination of good fishing, beautiful backcountry views, and a fairly short hike. Despite its popularity, the lake is large enough for everyone to find a slice of shoreline to call his or her own. More adventuresome hikers can bring a small raft or bellyboat (no motors, though) and relax on one of the three islands that give the lake its name. Unfortunately, overuse has led to the closure of Three Island Lake to camping within ¼-mile of its shore. This closure will allow the vegetation to recover. Be sure to read the Wilderness regulations carefully if you are planning to camp near Three Island Lake.

Hikers with a bit more time (and skill at reading maps and using a compass) can continue past Three Island Lake to Beaver

Three Island Lake.

Lake. Beaver Lake lies only ¼-mile off the Three Island Lake trail but lacks a defined trail to its shore. Fishing for brook trout is better at Beaver Lake than at Three Island Lake, though the fish tend to be smaller.

There are three different trailheads for the Three Island Lake Trail (#1163). To reach any of the three, take Routt County 129 north from Steamboat Springs for 17.4 miles to Forest Service Road 400 (Seedhouse Road). To reach the first trailhead, follow Road 400 approximately 9.2 miles to the Seedhouse Campground. The trail to Three Island Lake begins in the Seedhouse Campground across from campsite number 5. From the campground, the hike to Three Island Lake is 5 miles (one way).

To reach the other two trailheads, continue on Forest Service Road 400 an additional ⁷⁄₁₀-mile beyond Seedhouse Campground to Forest Service Road 443. Turn right (south) on Road 443. There are two trailheads for Three Island Lake along Road 443. The first is 1.2 miles beyond the intersection of Roads 400 and 443. The distance to Three Island Lake from this trailhead is about 4 miles. To shorten hiking distance to 3.5 miles, continue on Road 443 an additional 2 miles. A large Routt National Forest sign marks the final

Snow persists at Beaver Lake well into July.

trailhead (**Point A**) for Three Island Lake and Beaver Lake. The trail begins on the left (north) side of the road.

Begin hiking uphill on switchbacks through dense aspen and chokecherry. After ¼-mile, intersect the trail coming up from the campground (**Point B**). Turn right at the intersection and continue east. For the next ½-mile the trail slowly gains elevation. A break in the trees to the right at mile 1.25 reveals a view up a valley and the Dome in the distance. Many of the large aspen along the trail have names carved in them. If you feel inclined to leave your mark here, do so by joining the Wilderness Society, not by adding your name to the collection.

Two miles from the trailhead, Three Island Creek appears alongside the trail, which remains on the ridge above. One-half mile later, hike past a waterfall before switchbacking uphill for another ½-mile. Just above the switchbacks the trail drops back down along the creek. Three miles from the trailhead the trail enters the Mount Zirkel Wilderness. At mile 3.5, enter a large open meadow with a rocky hillside rising above it. Just beyond this meadow the trail reaches Three Island Lake (**Point C**).

Three Island Lake (9,878 feet, 23 acres) is one of the largest lakes in the wilderness. Appropriately, it features three islands complete with their own "miniature" forests. The best vantage point and photo perch is on the rocks above the south shore. Most of the overused campsites are along the forested north shore, which parallels the trail as it continues east to the Continental Divide. Both the eastern and southern shores are swampy in spots. Three Island Lake offers good fishing for small brook trout.

To continue to Beaver Lake, pick up the trail on the north side of Three Island Lake and head east. The trail beyond Three Island Lake is well defined but somewhat rocky and rough in places. It starts out level and features an abundance of yellow glacier lilies in early summer. At ½-mile, cross the inlet stream to Three Island Lake. Three-quarters of a mile from Three Island Lake, you enter a clearing brimming with glacier lilies and boulders. A quarter-mile past the clearing the trail comes up a ridge with the inlet creek to Three Island Lake on the left, then levels off and enters a meadow (**Point D**).

Because the trail from Three Island Lake does not lead directly to Beaver Lake and the turnoff to Beaver Lake is not marked, finding it takes a bit of skill. A couple of clues should help: 1. after entering the meadow, look for the small stream to the right of the trail that drains from Beaver Lake; 2. about ⅒-mile before the turnoff there will be a pond to the left of the trail; 3. keep looking between the trees to the right of the trail for a large bare-rock wall that rises above and behind Beaver Lake. The turnoff to Beaver Lake is about 1.25 miles from Three Island Lake. The trail to Beaver Lake is to the right of Beaver Lake's outlet stream and is not well defined where the outlet stream intersects the meadow but becomes more defined a couple of hundred feet up the hill. The hike from the meadow to Beaver Lake (**Point E**) is roughly ¼-mile. If you miss the turnoff and continue to follow the trail you will, after several more miles, end up at the Continental Divide.

Beaver Lake (10,340 feet, 7 acres) is not as popular as other lakes in this part of the Wilderness; thus it will not be unusual if you have the lake to yourself. The north, east, and south sides of the lake are surrounded by spruce and fir. The best campsites can be found on the eastern and northern shores. Beaver Lake offers excellent fishing for small (six- to eight-inch) but eager brook trout.

Dome Lake

Trailhead
> *North Lake Trailhead (#1164 to #1169)*

Starting elevation
> *8,460 feet*

Ending elevation
> *10,060 feet*

Distance (round trip)
> *11 miles*

Time required (round trip)
> *6 hours*

Rating
> *Difficult*

Maps
> *7.5' Mount Zirkel*
> *7.5' Mount Ethel*
> *Routt National Forest*

Main attractions
> *Rugged hike to a remote alpine lake; solitude; fishing in the South Fork Elk River on the way to the lake.*

Although the rewards of reaching Dome Lake are many, this hike is recommended for experienced hikers only. Listed as trail #1169 on the Routt National Forest map, the Dome Lake Trail is not maintained, and lack of visitor use makes it difficult to follow, especially in wet areas where the vegetation recovers quickly. Fortunately, the trail never wanders too far from the west side of the South Fork Elk River. The lake sits beneath the "Dome," an appropriately named landmark visible from the meadows along the route. You will remain headed in the right direction if you stay fairly close to the river and aim for the Dome.

To reach the trailhead, take Routt County 129 north from Steamboat Springs for 17.4 miles to Forest Service Road 400 (Seedhouse Road). Follow Road 400 for 9.9 miles and turn right on Forest Service Road 443. Continue on Road 443 for 5.3 miles until it dead-ends at the North Lake trailhead. The final 1.4 miles

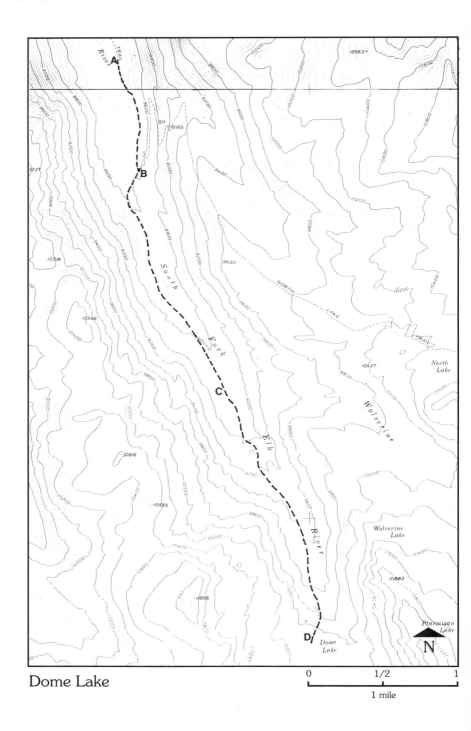

Dome Lake

0   1/2   1

1 mile

Crossing the South Fork Elk River on the Dome Lake Trail.

of Road 443 are rough but can be negotiated without four-wheel-drive.

The trail to Dome Lake starts from the North Lake trailhead (#1164) (**Point A**). The sign at the trailhead does not mention Dome Lake. The North Lake Trail begins in a mixture of spruce and fir and enters the Mount Zirkel Wilderness ¼-mile from the trailhead. Shortly after passing the Wilderness boundary, you will cross a small stream and begin to switchback up a slope. Complete the first switchback. As the trail heads away from the stream on the second switchback, it will fork (**Point B**). The right fork is the Dome Lake Trail (#1169), only ⅓-mile from the North Lake trailhead. The Dome Lake Trail immediately heads downhill and crosses the South Fork Elk River. The river can be quite high and cold, making the crossing bone-chilling and worthy of caution. Since this crossing is close to the trailhead, consider bringing along an old pair of tennis shoes to wear while crossing, and stash the shoes on the other side for your return trip.

After crossing the river the trail is quite distinct and winds through spruce and fir. Enter a meadow with views up the valley of the Dome about ⅓-mile after the river crossing. Continue into a second, larger meadow containing numerous downed trees. The trail is difficult to follow in these wet areas and splits about halfway across this meadow. It is possible to continue straight ahead toward the trees at the far end of the meadow, but this route requires climbing over several large downed trees. An alternate route involves bearing right toward the slope above the meadow, avoiding the downed trees, and rejoining the trail in the trees beyond the meadow. Once through the meadow the trail becomes distinct again in the wooded section.

The trail disappears in a forested area 1.4 miles from the trailhead. Your best option is to follow the river closely until you relocate the trail. The trail enters another meadow containing many downed trees at mile 2 (**Point C**). Shortly after entering the meadow, head uphill to the right and pass through a gap between a group of trees and the steep slope bordering the western edge of the meadow. Drop back down at the far side of the meadow and follow the trail as it enters the trees. From this point on, with the exception of a few small wet meadows, the trail is fairly easy to follow as it meanders southward within earshot of the South Fork Elk River.

Four miles from the trailhead the South Fork Elk River is visible cascading through a narrow canyon. For the next ½-mile the trail follows the river and rises gradually. At mile 5, a talus slope to the right marks the beginning of the final, arduous ascent to the lake. Climb steeply for the next ½-mile and arrive at Dome Lake (**Point D**) 5.5 miles from the trailhead.

Dome Lake (10,060 feet, 11 acres) is strikingly beautiful, with the Dome rising impressively beyond the south shore. Other jagged peaks surround the Dome and provide a spectacular backdrop for photographers. Despite the lake's remote location, fishing at Dome Lake is only fair. The lake contains Colorado River cutthroat trout, the native trout of Colorado's Western Slope. These are indeed beautiful fish, and catching one in such a pristine setting is a memorable experience. Most range from eight to twelve inches, but occasional lunkers exceeding five pounds lurk in the depths.

Dome Lake with the Dome rising above it to the south.

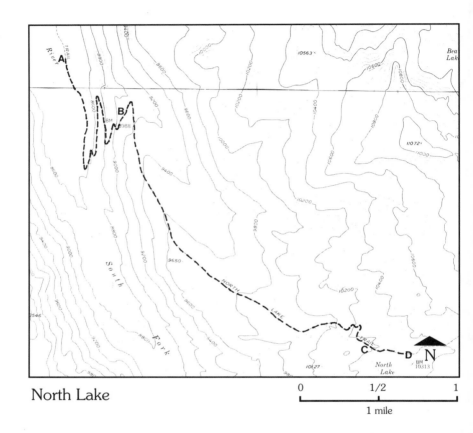

North Lake

0   1/2   1

1 mile

North Lake

Trailhead
>   North Lake Trailhead (#1164)

Starting elevation
>   8,460 feet

Ending elevation
>   10,313 feet

Distance (round trip)
>   8 miles

Time required (round trip)
>   4 hours

Rating
>   Moderate/Difficult

Maps
>   7.5' Mount Zirkel
>   7.5' Mount Ethel
>   Routt National Forest

Main attractions
>   Good fishing for pan-sized brook trout; ideal stopover for
>   multiday trips to Wolverine Basin or along the Continental
>   Divide.

North Lake lies at the end of an uphill 4-mile hike, gaining
nearly 2,000 feet in elevation from the trailhead. Although not as
scenic as the more popular lakes to the north (Three Island Lake,
Gold Creek Lake, and Gilpin Lake), North Lake does offer good
fishing and more solitude. North Lake can also be incorporated into
a multiday loop hike that includes the Wolverine Basin lakes and the
Wyoming Trail along the Continental Divide.

To reach the trailhead, take Routt County 129 north from
Steamboat Springs for 17.4 miles to Forest Service Road 400
(Seedhouse Road). Follow Road 400 for 9.9 miles and turn right on
Forest Service Road 443. Continue on Road 443 for 5.3 miles until
it dead-ends at the North Lake trailhead (#1164) (**Point A**). The
final 1.4 miles of Road 443 are rough, but can be negotiated
without four-wheel drive.

North Lake.

The North Lake Trail begins in a mixture of spruce and fir and quickly enters the Mount Zirkel Wilderness. Shortly after passing the Wilderness boundary, cross a stream and begin to switchback up a slope. As the trail heads away from the stream on the second switchback, a fork to the right leads to Dome Lake. Stay to the left on the main trail, which becomes rocky and rough. Continue to climb steep switchbacks up the hill for another ¾-mile. The trail reaches the top of the ridge 1 mile from the trailhead (**Point B**) and levels off. However, within ⅒-mile, the trail again climbs uphill more gradually along a ridge between the South Fork Elk River to the west and an unnamed drainage to the east. For the next 2 miles the trail continues to slowly gain elevation. Three miles from the trailhead a break in the trees provides a view to the southwest of the peak appropriately known as the Dome. About ½-mile beyond this viewpoint, enter a short series of steep switchbacks, then head along a ridge above a ravine and pass to the left of a large open meadow. At the far end of this meadow an unsigned trail-fork to the right (**Point C**) leads south to the Wolverine Basin Lakes. Stay on the main trail at this fork and ¼-mile later you arrive at North Lake (**Point D**).

North Lake (10,313 feet, 6 acres) is a pretty lake, though not spectacular by Mount Zirkel Wilderness standards. Its shores are mostly open, providing an ideal opportunity to fly-fish for pan-sized brook trout. North Lake is well located to serve as a stopover for an extended backpacking trek. The best campsites can be found in the trees near the western and southern shores.

Those hikers with additional energy or plans for backpacking can follow the North Lake Trail another mile beyond the lake to its intersection with the Wyoming Trail (#1101) on the Continental Divide. Another option is to head ¼-mile back toward the trailhead and follow the Wolverine Basin Trail to Wolverine Lake, Ptarmigan Lake, and Pristine Lake (see page 51).

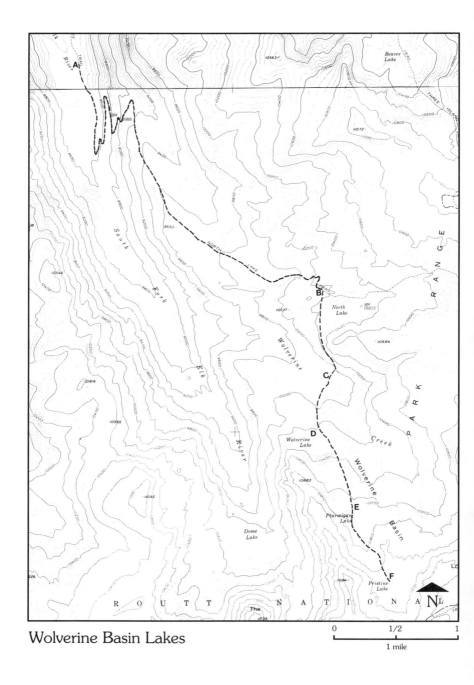

Wolverine Basin Lakes

Wolverine Basin Lakes

Trailhead

> North Lake Trailhead (#1164)

Starting elevation

> 8,460 feet

Ending elevation

> Wolverine Lake: 10,284 feet
>
> Ptarmigan Lake: 10,699 feet
>
> Pristine Lake: 11,040 feet

Distance (round trip)

> Wolverine Lake: 10 miles
>
> Ptarmigan Lake: 11 miles
>
> Pristine Lake: 12 miles

Time required (round trip)

> Wolverine Lake: 5 hours
>
> Ptarmigan Lake: 6.5 hours
>
> Pristine Lake: 8 hours

Rating

> Moderate/Difficult

Maps

> 7.5′ Mount Zirkel
>
> 7.5′ Mount Ethel
>
> Routt National Forest

Main attractions

> Seldom-visited, rarely fished lakes in the heart of the Mount
> Zirkel Wilderness; excellent backcountry camping.

Tucked away in their own secluded valley, the Wolverine Basin lakes (Wolverine, Ptarmigan, and Pristine) offer backpackers or ambitious day hikers an ideal getaway. All three lakes offer good fishing: Wolverine and Ptarmigan for plump cutthroat trout and "cutbows" (hybrid cross of rainbow and cutthroat trout), and Pristine for pan-size brook trout. Wolverine Basin lakes are accessible from the north via the North Lake Trail (#1164), or the south via the Wyoming Trail (#1101) from Buffalo Pass. The shorter northern route is described below. Wolverine Lake can be reached reasonably

Wolverine Lake. The rim of Wolverine Basin can be seen in the background.

in a day, but we recommend spending several days to explore this remote valley. From Pristine Lake it is a short but steep scramble to the Continental Divide and the Wyoming Trail, which opens up a wide array of other nearby destinations.

To reach the trailhead, take Routt County 129 north from Steamboat Springs for 17.4 miles to Forest Service Road 400 (Seedhouse Road). Follow Road 400 for 9.9 miles and turn right on Forest Service Road 443. Continue on Road 443 for 5.3 miles until it dead-ends at the North Lake trailhead (**Point A**). The final 1.4 miles of Road 443 are rough but can be negotiated without four-wheel-drive.

To reach Wolverine Basin, follow the North Lake Trail (#1164) as it climbs uphill from the trailhead. The first mile is mostly continuous switchbacks as the trail rises well above the South Fork Elk River valley. Over the next 2 miles continue to gain elevation at a more gradual pace. About 3.5 miles beyond the trailhead, begin a series of short, steep switchbacks. Shortly after you crest the switchbacks, a large grassy meadow comes into view to the right of the trail. At the far edge of this meadow the trail to Wolverine Basin lakes is faintly visible to the right (south) (**Point B**). The turnoff to

Wolverine Basin lakes is not marked, so be alert. The Routt National Forest map does not show a trail to Wolverine Basin, and this trail is not maintained. If you inadvertently miss the turnoff, you will arrive at North Lake ¼-mile farther up the North Lake Trail and there realize your mistake.

The trail to Wolverine Basin lakes heads south along the eastern edge of the meadow. The trail through the meadow is faint in spots but becomes very distinct once it enters the trees about 500 feet from the turnoff. Shortly, descend steeply and cross the outlet stream from North Lake. Arrive at Wolverine Creek (**Point C**), which drains all three Wolverine Basin lakes, ¾-mile after leaving the North Lake Trail. About ½-mile beyond Wolverine Creek, climb steeply up to a ridge that reveals the inviting green waters of Wolverine Lake (**Point D**) shimmering in the basin below.

Wolverine Lake (10,284 feet, 7 acres) is surrounded on three sides by a mixture of mature spruce and fir trees. The open south-eastern shore features a long sandy beach, which furnishes an ideal spot to relax after the long hike. The northwest shore offers impressive views across the lake of the barren ridgeline that forms the western edge of Wolverine Basin. Wolverine Lake contains cut-throat and cutbow trout that grow to sixteen inches. Backcountry campsites are located in the trees on the eastern and northern sides of the lake.

To continue to Ptarmigan Lake, rejoin the main trail above the southeastern edge of Wolverine Lake. Just beyond Wolverine Lake you will pass a small overgrown pond on the right. A small rock cairn marks a faint trail leading into the trees to the right, 350 feet beyond the pond. This is the trail to Ptarmigan Lake. Wind through the trees for almost ½-mile to a wet meadow at the base of a steep incline. To the far left is a sheer rock face, left center is the outlet stream from Ptarmigan Lake tumbling rapidly over rocks, and straight ahead is a forested slope. A rock cairn at the base of the slope marks the spot where you can pick up the trail. The trail becomes very distinct as it switchbacks up the final forested pitch to Ptarmigan Lake (**Point E**).

Ptarmigan Lake (10,699 feet, 7 acres) is similar to Wolverine Lake in size and appearance. The deep southwest shore offers excellent fishing for meaty cutthroat trout. Campsites are available on the eastern side of the lake.

We highly recommend continuing from Ptarmigan Lake to

Pristine Lake, photographed from the Continental Divide below Lost Ranger Peak.

starkly beautiful Pristine Lake. The trail is easy to spot as it
meanders up the hillside above the south end of Ptarmigan Lake.
At the top of the slope the trail fades and is virtually nonexistent for
the remainder of the route to Pristine Lake. Fortunately, the rest of
the hike to Pristine Lake is above timberline in a confined valley, so
it is impossible to lose your way. Simply head toward the reddish
band of rock above the green-gray cliffs that form the southern wall
of Wolverine Basin. In less than 1 mile beyond Ptarmigan Lake, you
will arrive at Pristine Lake (**Point F**).

Pristine Lake (11,040 feet, 10 acres) lies in a spectacular setting
well above timberline. Its deep waters are an incredible emerald
green. The southern shoreline features large rocks jutting directly
from the water's edge. The views from these rocks looking north to
Mount Zirkel and the Sawtooth Range are magnificent. Pristine Lake
supports a healthy population of small (eight- to twelve-inch) brook
trout.

The Wyoming Trail (#1101) along the Continental Divide lies
only ½-mile above Pristine Lake. It is possible to scramble over the
rocks and up the slope southeast of Pristine Lake to a saddle on the
Continental Divide below Lost Ranger Peak.

Lake Diana

Trailhead
> *Main Fork Trail (#1152) at Diamond Park Trailhead*

Starting elevation
> *8,800 feet*

Ending elevation
> *10,268 feet*

Distance (round trip)
> *From Diamond Park Trailhead: 8 miles*
> *From Trail Creek: 12 miles*

Time required (round trip)
> *From Diamond Park Trailhead: 4 hours*
> *From Trail Creek: 6 hours*

Rating
> *Moderate*

Maps
> *7.5' Mount Zirkel*
> *7.5' Farwell Mountain*
> *Routt National Forest*

Main attractions
> *Classically beautiful alpine lake; excellent fishing for native cutthroat trout; opportunity to combine with other destinations into a multiday backpacking loop.*

Few people venture to Lake Diana due to the length of the hike and the difficult access to the Diamond Park trailhead (a four-wheel-drive vehicle is required). Those who are able to make the trip are not disappointed. The hike includes unsurpassed views of the Sawtooth Range and superb fishing for native cutthroat trout at Lake Diana. In addition to being a delightful day-hike destination, Lake Diana can be combined with hikes to other lakes (Gem Lake, West Fork Lake, Seven Lakes) as part of a multiday backpacking trip.

To reach the trailhead, take Routt County 129 north from Steamboat Springs for 17.4 miles to Forest Service Road 400 (Seedhouse Road). Follow Forest Service Road 400 for 9.1 miles and turn left (north) on Forest Service Road 431. Road 431 is a

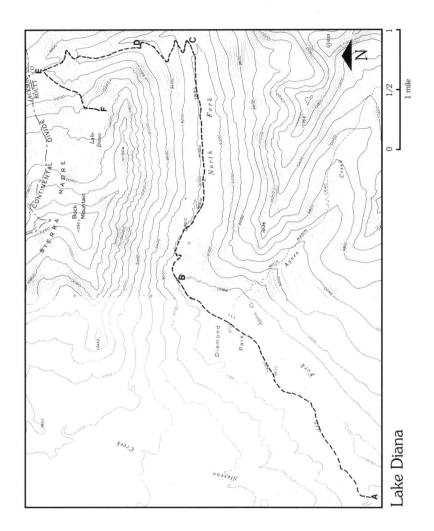

Lake Diana

Looking south to the Sawtooth Range from the Main Fork Trail on the way to Lake Diana.

deeply rutted, primitive, four-wheel-drive road to the Diamond Park trailhead. Follow Road 431 north 4.8 miles to a fork. Go right at the fork, as the sign directs, toward Manzanares Lake. Follow this right fork for another ⅔₁₀-mile. At this point, depending on the time of the year and your vehicle clearance, you may or may not be able to cross Trail Creek, which flows over the road. If your vehicle cannot cross Trail Creek, begin the hike to Lake Diana on foot. The following hike description begins at the Trail Creek crossing.

After crossing Trail Creek (**Point A**), the road splits into several forks. The fork farthest left (north) is Road 431. Remain on 431 as it continues toward the Diamond Park trailhead through open sagebrush-covered terrain. The road crosses Stevens Creek less than 1 mile beyond Trail Creek. Two miles from the Trail Creek crossing the road ends at the Diamond Park trailhead (**Point B**).

To reach Lake Diana, take the Main Fork Trail (#1152). Only ⅒-mile from the trailhead the trail enters the Mount Zirkel Wilderness and gradually climbs through sagebrush, aspen, spruce, and fir. One mile from the trailhead, drop alongside the lazily flowing North Fork of the Encampment River. Those with fishing gear will be

Lake Diana, photographed from the rock outcrop above the northwest shore.

hard-pressed to pass by the deep pools without casting. After moving away from the stream and into lush spruce and fir, the trail turns north upon reaching the Encampment River (**Point C**), about 2.2 miles from the trailhead. Take a deep breath and begin a series of long switchbacks that lead away from the North Fork Encampment River. Admire the spectacular view of the Sawtooth Range to the southeast as you pause to rest along the switchbacks. At the end of the switchbacks wind your way to the edge of a high cliff (**Point D**) that overlooks the Main Fork Encampment River.

After descending to the ridge to join the Encampment River, cross the outlet stream from Lake Diana. Resist the temptation to follow the outlet stream up to the lake; continue on the Main Fork Trail. From the crossing, climb steadily ½-mile to a fork (**Point E**). A sign at the fork indicates the trail to Lake Diana on the left. The Lake Diana Trail passes through two wet meadows before turning steeply uphill along the right side of the outlet stream. The trail is distinct but not well maintained. After passing through two more wet meadows and crossing the outlet stream, arrive at Lake Diana (**Point F**), ¾-mile from the Main Fork Trail and 4 miles from the Diamond Park trailhead.

Lake Diana (10,268 feet, 9 acres) is a classically beautiful alpine lake featuring a sheer rock face rising abruptly from its north shore. The lake is perched on a shelf high above the floor of the Encampment River Valley. The deep water along the north shore is an impressive shade of blue-green. Unlike many nearby lakes, which contain only brook trout, Lake Diana features excellent fishing for eight- to twelve-inch cutthroat trout. The fish in Lake Diana are a fairly pure population of native Colorado River cutthroat trout, the only trout native to western Colorado. Several campsites are available for those visiting Lake Diana as part of a backpacking loop.

The Main Fork Trail continues north from the Lake Diana turnoff, bypassing spur trails to Gem Lake, Seven Lakes, and Swamp Park before arriving at the Hog Park Guard Station outside the northern boundary of the Mount Zirkel Wilderness.

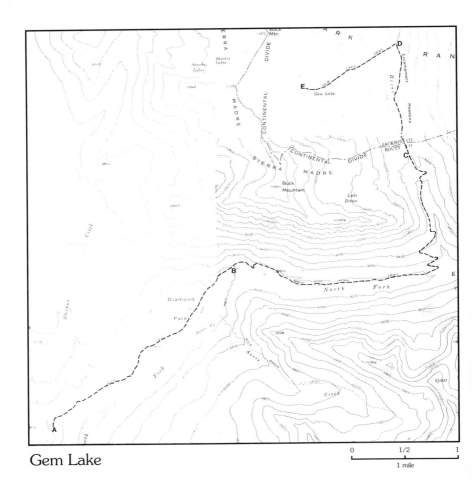

Gem Lake

Gem Lake

Trailhead
> *Main Fork Trail (#1152) at Diamond Park Trailhead*

Starting elevation
> *8,800 feet*

Ending elevation
> *10,160 feet*

Distance (round trip)
> *From Diamond Park Trailhead: 10 miles*
> *From Trail Creek: 14 miles*

Time required (round trip)
> *From Diamond Park Trailhead: 5 hours*
> *From Trail Creek: 7 hours*

Rating
> *Moderate*

Maps
> *7.5' Farwell Mountain*
> *7.5' West Fork Lake*
> *7.5' Davis Peak*
> *Routt National Forest*

Main attractions
> *Remote lake in rugged surroundings; good fishing; ideal stopover on a multiday backpacking loop.*

Gem Lake is a ruggedly beautiful alpine lake nestled beneath the sheer face of Buck Mountain. Although the lake is accessible from several trailheads, the easiest route (described below) is from Diamond Park, which involves a very rough drive to the trailhead. Gem Lake is centrally located in the northern portion of the Mount Zirkel Wilderness and can easily be combined with trips to other nearby lakes (West Fork Lake, Seven Lakes, Lake Diana) as part of a backpacking loop hike.

To reach the trailhead, take Routt County 129 north from Steamboat Springs for 17.4 miles to Forest Service Road 400 (Seedhouse Road). Follow Forest Service Road 400 for 9.1 miles and turn left (north) on Forest Service Road 431. Road 431 is a

Sheer rock wall rising above the western shore of Gem Lake.

deeply rutted, primitive, four-wheel-drive road to the Diamond Park trailhead. Take Road 431 north 4.8 miles to a fork in the road. Go right at the fork, as the sign directs, toward Manzanares Lake. Follow the fork for another $\frac{2}{10}$-mile. At this point, depending on the time of year and your vehicle clearance, you may or may not be able to cross Trail Creek, which flows over the road. If your vehicle cannot cross Trail Creek, begin the hike to Gem Lake on foot.

From Trail Creek (**Point A**), follow Road 431 for 2 miles to the Diamond Park trailhead (**Point B**). To reach Gem Lake, follow the hike narration for Lake Diana on page 55. Just over 3 miles from the Diamond Park trailhead, continue straight on the Main Fork Trail past the turnoff (**Point C**) to Lake Diana. The Main Fork Trail proceeds north through Encampment Meadows alongside the Encampment River. Look for a large rock cairn on the right side of the trail 1 mile beyond the Lake Diana turnoff. The Gem Lake Trail (**Point D**) is faintly visible to the left, about 30 feet before you reach the cairn. Immediately cross the Encampment River where a sign marks the Gem Lake Trail (#1152-A). Climb steeply for ½-mile to a meadow filled with wildflowers and spectacular views of snowclad Buck Mountain. Continue through the meadow (signposts mark the way) into the trees for the final short climb to Gem Lake (**Point E**).

The western edge of Gem Lake (10,160 feet, 7 acres) is dominated by a sheer rock wall rising above the clear blue water. The lake offers excellent fishing for brook trout to eleven inches. Campsites are available on the north side of the lake or in the forest alongside the meadow below the lake.

Gem Lake can also be reached from the Hog Park trailhead or the Big Creek trailhead, but it is at least an overnight hike from either. From Hog Park, follow the Main Fork Trail alongside the Encampment River for 11.5 miles to the Gem Lake turnoff. Gem Lake lies about 9 miles from the Big Creek trailhead via the Big Creek Trail (#1125) to the Main Fork Trail.

Destinations in the Eastern Mount Zirkel Wilderness

Lakes, waterfalls, and mountain passes beckon hikers to the eastern portion of the Mount Zirkel Wilderness. The eastern Wilderness offers a wide range of trails for hikers of all abilities. The two largest lakes in the Wilderness, Rainbow and Roxy Ann, lie east of the Continental Divide, and fishermen seeking lake trout (mackinaw) have three lakes in which to try their luck: Katherine, Twin, and Blue.

This section includes short hikes to Big Creek Falls, Newcomb Park, and Lake Katherine that are suitable for families. Longer hikes to some of our favorite Wilderness destinations (Rainbow Lakes, Slide Lakes, and Roxy Ann Lake) are also described. West Fork Lake, Twin Lakes, and Blue Lake are ideal backpacking escapes featuring rugged scenery, good backcountry campsites, and fishing opportunities.

Directions to the trailheads in this section are given from Walden, the largest town to the east of the Mount Zirkel Wilderness.

West Fork Lake Loop

Trailhead
>   West Fork Trailhead (#1153)

Starting elevation
>   8,374 feet

Ending elevation
>   9,305 feet

Distance
>   West Fork Lake via West Fork Trail (one way): 7 miles
>   West Fork Lake via Main Fork Trail (one way): 9 miles
>   Entire loop: 16 miles

Time required
>   West Fork Lake (one way): 4 hours
>   Entire loop: 8 hours

Rating
>   Easy

Maps
>   7.5' West Fork Lake
>   7.5' Davis Peak
>   Routt National Forest

Main attractions
>   An easy backpacking loop hike through mountain meadows
>   to a high mountain lake; good fishing.

The loop trail to West Fork Lake offers a lengthy but level excursion into the northern Mount Zirkel Wilderness. West Fork Lake sits at the halfway point of the loop, making it an ideal camping spot for a two-or-more-day backpack. The trail parallels the West Fork of the Encampment River all the way to the lake; the return loop follows the Main Fork of the Encampment River. West Fork Lake is lower in elevation than most lakes in the Mount Zirkel Wilderness, making it accessible earlier in the summer (late June/ early July in most years).

To reach the trailhead, take State Highway 125 north from Walden to Cowdrey. In Cowdrey, turn left (west) on Jackson County 6 toward Lake John. The pavement ends after 5 miles and

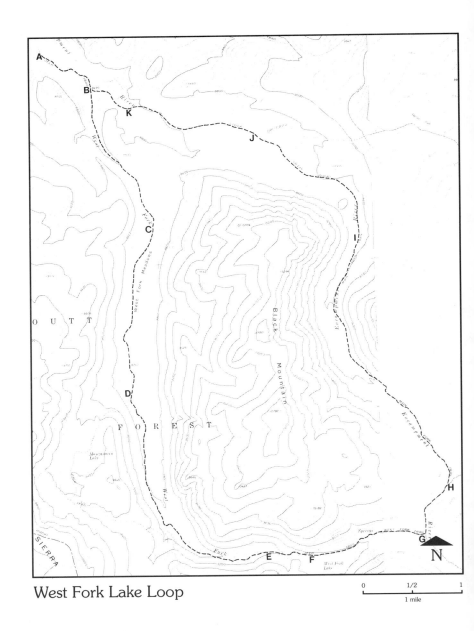

West Fork Lake Loop

the road becomes an all-weather dirt road. Continue past the turnoff to Lake John and Big Creek Lakes and follow the signs to Hog Park Reservoir. Enter the Routt National Forest 19 miles from Cowdrey, where the road becomes Forest Service Road 80. Stay on Road 80 for 16 miles. Immediately after crossing the Encampment River turn left at the sign for Hog Park Guard Station. The road to the guard station is rough but passable for most vehicles. You can park at the guard station or carefully continue another ¾-mile along the road to a parking area at the trailhead (**Point A**). The area surrounding the trailhead offers several good campsites, so arriving in the evening prior to a morning trail departure is an option.

The first part of the West Fork Trail (#1153) follows an old jeep road. After only 300 yards you encounter the first of three crossings of the West Fork Encampment River. There are no bridges on this loop hike (and plenty of river crossings), so an extra pair of old tennis shoes for the crossings will come in handy. The river crossings are fairly simple (knee deep), but require caution, especially in early summer when the rivers run high and cold with snowmelt. The trail forks (**Point B**) ¼-mile past the first river crossing; take the right fork and climb gradually through spruce and fir interspersed with meadows. After another mile the jeep road levels and becomes a single trail. Shortly after a second river crossing, 3 miles from the trailhead, the trail enters West Fork Meadows (**Point C**). The meadows can be swampy, especially early in the season. The trail through the meadows fades in and out but is marked by signposts to guide you in the right direction.

About ¾-mile after reentering the forest on the far side of West Fork Meadows, a sign marks the trail (#1204) (**Point D**) to Manzanares Lake. For those with extra time or energy, the steep trip to Manzanares Lake can be made into a 2.5-mile loop that rejoins the West Fork Trail about 1.5 miles from this junction. The lake offers excellent campsites near its northern shore and occasionally yields a good-size brook trout. Unless you have time to spare, we recommend bypassing the trip to Manzanares Lake and continuing on the West Fork Trail toward West Fork Lake.

Six and one-half miles from the trailhead, enter the Mount Zirkel Wilderness (**Point E**). One-half mile past the wilderness boundary you arrive at West Fork Lake (**Point F**) (9,305 feet, 13 acres). Good campsites can be found in the trees on the lake's north shore and on the bluffs overlooking the lake on the northwest

Overlooking West Fork Lake from the bluff above its northwest shore.

side. The south shore is heavily forested and drops sharply to the edge of the lake. West Fork Lake contains numerous brook trout in the eight- to twelve-inch range.

To complete the loop hike and return to the trailhead, rejoin the West Fork Trail on the north side of the lake and head east. About 1 mile after leaving West Fork Lake, the West Fork Trail intersects the Main Fork Trail (#1152) (**Point G**). Turn left (north) on the Main Fork Trail toward Hog Park. Shortly, a sign indicates that you are leaving the Mount Zirkel Wilderness (**Point H**). This point also marks the junction of the Main Fork Trail and the Stump Park Trail; take the left fork and remain on the Main Fork Trail. This trail junction is difficult to spot and is without a sign. The left fork (the one you want to take) is obscured by an uprooted tree, so be alert.

After leaving the wilderness, gradually descend through the forest and cross the Encampment River. You will arrive at an over- look above the Encampment River with Black Mountain rising on the west side of the river (**Point I**). This is an ideal spot to relax before the final leg of the hike. Two miles past the overlook the trail intersects the Center Stock Driveway Trail (**Point J**) in a meadow. Bear left and continue on the Center Stock Driveway before

The Main Fork of the Encampment River.

descending to a final crossing of the Encampment River (**Point K**).
Follow the rock cairns on the edge of the river to the spot where
crossing is easiest and the stream banks have been eroded by the
pounding of cattle hooves. Immediately after crossing, turn left and
look for a rock cairn to help you relocate the trail. Head directly
away from the river and stay to the right at the indistinct trail fork
about 200 feet past the river crossing. The Center Stock Driveway
rejoins the West Fork Trail ½-mile past the crossing (**Point B**).
Follow the West Fork Trail back to the trailhead.

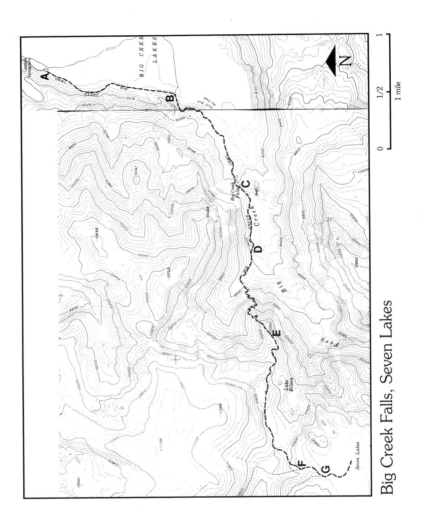

Big Creek Falls, Seven Lakes

Big Creek Falls, Seven Lakes

Trailhead
>Big Creek Trailhead (#1125)

Starting elevation
>9,000 feet

Ending elevation
>Big Creek Falls: 9,230 feet
>Seven Lakes: 10,773 feet

Distance (round trip)
>Big Creek Falls: 5 miles
>Seven Lakes: 9 miles

Time required (round trip)
>Big Creek Falls: 2.5 hours
>Seven Lakes: 5 hours

Rating
>Big Creek Falls: Easy
>Seven Lakes: Moderate

Maps
>7.5' Davis Peak
>7.5' Pearl
>Routt National Forest

Main attractions
>Scenic, level hike to a picturesque waterfall; opportunity to continue hiking to a group of high lakes in an open alpine meadow.

The trail to Big Creek Falls affords a leisurely hike past Upper Big Creek Lake to a pretty waterfall just inside the Mount Zirkel Wilderness boundary. More ambitious day hikers or backpackers can continue up the trail past the falls to Seven Lakes Basin. The trail leaves from the Big Creek Lakes Campground along the shores of Lower Big Creek Lake in the Routt National Forest, just outside the northeast border of the Mount Zirkel Wilderness. The campground is a great place to spend a few days relaxing and fishing for rainbow, brown, and brook trout in the 350-acre lower lake.

Big Creek Falls.

To reach the Big Creek trailhead, take State Highway 125 north from Walden to Cowdrey. In Cowdrey, turn left (west) on Jackson County 6 toward Lake John. The pavement ends after 5 miles and the road becomes an all-weather dirt road. Continue straight past the Lake John turnoff and turn left (south) on Forest Service Road 600, 18.5 miles from Cowdrey. Stay on Forest Service Road 600 for 6 miles and keep to the right at the entrance to Big Creek Lakes Campground. Once in the campground, follow the trailhead symbols ⁹/₁₀-mile to the Big Creek trailhead (**Point A**).

Due to its popularity and use as an interpretive/nature trail, the first section of the Big Creek Falls Trail is wide and level. Numbered posts along the trail refer to points of interest that are described in a booklet that can be obtained at the trailhead. The trail passes through a mixed forest of spruce, fir, lodgepole pine, and an occasional aspen. The trail forks 1.5 miles from the trailhead (**Point B**). The left fork leads a short distance to Upper Big Creek Lake; take the right fork and continue past the lake toward Big Creek Falls. About 1 mile past the fork the trail enters the Mount Zirkel Wilderness. Here the rush of Big Creek Falls is audible in the background. Just beyond the Wilderness boundary the falls come into view (**Point C**). A short, steep trail descends to the base of the falls, which divide into twin cascades as Big Creek plunges over a jumble of large, angular rocks. The area below the falls is an enchanting spot to enjoy a bite to eat.

If time and energy remain, rejoin the trail as it climbs up and away from Big Creek on the way to Seven Lakes. About ¼-mile beyond the falls the trail drops beside the creek and remains level for the next ½-mile. It then gradually begins to steepen (**Point D**), which is only a mild precursor of things to come. The trail enters a long series of switchbacks 1 mile beyond the falls, gaining 750 feet in ½-mile. Be sure to take frequent rests and enjoy the expansive views back down the valley toward Big Creek Lakes and south to Red Elephant Mountain. After passing over the top of a knoll at 10,350 feet (**Point E**), the trail levels out as it continues west toward Seven Lakes. After passing through several open meadows, reach the first of two signed forks (**Point F**). Take the left fork toward Encampment Meadows. Shortly thereafter the trail forks again; take the left fork to Seven Lakes. Just past the fork, top the ridge and enter Seven Lakes Basin (**Point G**).

Unlike most lakes in the Mount Zirkel Wilderness, Seven Lakes

Fishing for cutthroat trout at Seven Lakes.

are situated in open, mostly treeless country. Backpackers will find numerous campsites scattered among the trees surrounding the open meadows. All but one of the lakes are shallow and some dry up in late summer to early fall. The largest and deepest lake can be reached by following the discernible path eastward as it winds around the smaller lakes. The large lake (10,773 feet, 14 acres) offers fair fishing for cutthroat trout to fourteen inches.

The Big Creek Trail continues west 2 miles where it intersects the Main Fork Trail (#1152) at the Encampment River. Gem Lake and Lake Diana lie south of this intersection off the Main Fork Trail. Hiking north along the Main Fork Trail leads to the West Fork Trail and West Fork Lake.

Lake Katherine, Bighorn Lake

Trailhead
> *Lake Katherine Trailhead (#1129) on Forest Service Road 640 (Lone Pine Road)*

Starting elevation
> *8,960 feet*

Ending elevation
> *Lake Katherine: 9,859 feet*
> *Bighorn Lake: 10,106 feet*

Distance (round trip)
> *Lake Katherine: 4 miles*
> *Bighorn Lake: 6 miles*

Time required (round trip)
> *Lake Katherine: 2 hours*
> *Bighorn Lake: 3.5 hours*

Rating
> *Easy/Moderate*

Maps
> *7.5' or 15' Mount Ethel*
> *7.5' or 15' Pearl*
> *Routt National Forest*

Main attractions
> *Short hikes to scenic mountain lakes with good fishing; easy road access.*

The trail to Lake Katherine and Bighorn Lake provides a quick escape into the Mount Zirkel Wilderness. Both lakes can be reached in a half-day and both reward hikers with rugged alpine beauty. Due to easy road access and short trail distance, Lake Katherine and Bighorn Lake are popular destinations.

To reach the Lake Katherine trailhead, take Highway 14 east from Walden. About ¼-mile outside of town turn right (west) on Jackson County 12. Watch for a wide array of birds on the fenceposts lining Jackson County 12. After about 5 miles, take the right fork (still Jackson County 12) toward Lake John. After 2.5 miles stay left on Jackson County 12, after 2 more miles stay to the right,

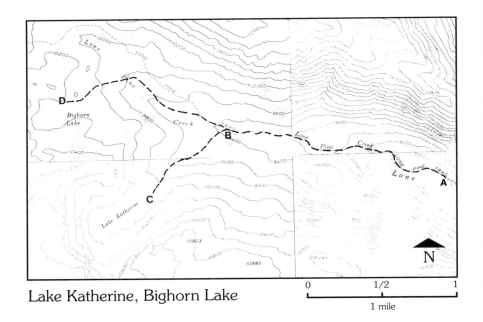

Lake Katherine, Bighorn Lake

Fog-shrouded peaks surrounding Lake Katherine. The majority of the lake is out of view to the right.

then continue an additional 2 miles. At the "T" in the road turn left on Jackson County 16. From this point on, the roads are all-weather dirt roads that are rough in a few spots but do not require four-wheel-drive. Pass through the Lone Pine Ranch and enter the Routt National Forest (Road 640) 5 miles from the T. The trailhead is 2.5 miles from the forest boundary and is marked by a sign at the end of the road (**Point A**). Several campsites are available near the road after it enters the forest and at the trailhead.

The trail to Lake Katherine meanders gradually uphill through spruce and fir trees and an occasional meadow. After ¾-mile, enter the Mount Zirkel Wilderness. Once inside the Wilderness boundary, the trail winds up and down through mature spruce and fir; intermittent meadows provide beautiful views of the surrounding mountains. The vegetation surrounding the trail is very lush and green; this part of the Wilderness gets plenty of rainfall. After passing a large boulder field on the right, head downhill to the left. A sign indicates a faint trail to the right that leads to the Continental Divide; stay to the left on the main trail. The trail forks again (**Point B**) 1.5 miles from the trailhead.

The left fork gains 450 feet in elevation in ¾-mile on the way to Lake Katherine (the right fork leads to Bighorn Lake). The trail to Lake Katherine almost immediately intersects a creek. There is no bridge here and high water makes a dry crossing difficult. To cross the creek, follow a trail leading upstream (right) about 200 feet to a large, solid log crossing. After the log crossing, immediately rejoin the Lake Katherine Trail. Climb steadily for ½-mile up to the lake (**Point C**). An old rock-and-cement arch over the outlet stream is all that remains of a dam that washed out in 1961.

Lake Katherine (9,859 feet, 23 acres) is a large, deep lake that contains lake trout and brook trout. Although it is usually a day-hike destination, good campsites are available in the trees on the northeast side of the lake.

To reach Bighorn Lake, continue straight (right) at the Lake Katherine Trail fork (**Point B**). From the fork, head uphill about 1 mile to Bighorn Lake (**Point D**). The final ½-mile to the lake is quite steep.

Bighorn Lake (10,106 feet, 14 acres) is forested on the north and south shores while the west end of the lake is very rocky. Fishing at Bighorn Lake can be quite good for cutthroat trout to twenty inches. Good campsites are located in the trees on the northeast side of the lake.

Bighorn Lake, with the Continental Divide rising in the distant background.

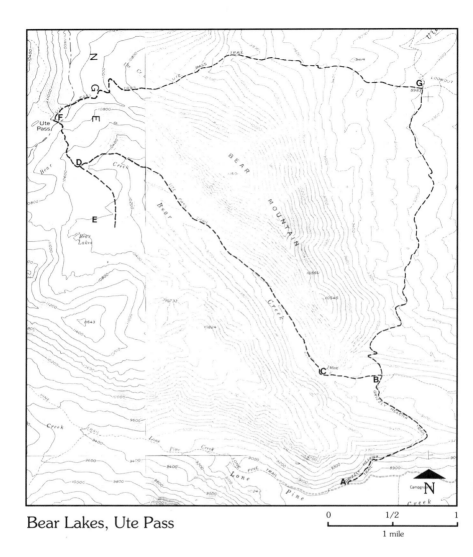

Bear Lakes, Ute Pass

Bear Lakes, Ute Pass

Trailhead

> Grizzly-Helena Trailhead (#1126) on Forest Service
> Road 640 (Lone Pine Road)

Starting elevation

> 8,870 feet

Ending elevation

> Bear Lakes: 10,343 feet
> Ute Pass: 11,000 feet

Distance (round trip)

> Bear Lakes: 11 miles
> Ute Pass: 11 miles
> Ute Pass Loop: 13.5 miles

Time required (round trip)

> Bear Lakes: 6 hours
> Ute Pass: 6 hours
> Ute Pass Loop: 7.5 hours

Rating

> Moderate

Maps

> 7.5' Pitchpine Mountain
> 7.5' Boettcher Lake
> 7.5' Mount Zirkel
> Routt National Forest

Main attractions

> Remote alpine lakes in a beautiful setting; trail
> bypasses an old mining site; good fishing for
> cutthroat trout.

Bear Lakes are beautiful, deep alpine lakes tucked in a rugged basin below Ute Pass. Despite their picturesque setting, these lakes are fairly remote and are seldom visited. Strong hikers can reach the lakes in a half-day and still have adequate time to fish for a few hours before returning to the trailhead. The lakes can also be visited by backpackers, although the isolated nature of Bear Lakes leaves backpackers with few nearby hiking alternatives aside from Ute Pass.

Ute Pass lies only ½-mile past the Bear Lakes turnoff and provides access to the lake basins and peaks surrounding Mount Zirkel.

To reach the Grizzly-Helena trailhead, take Highway 14 east from Walden. About ¼-mile outside of town turn right (west) on Jackson County 12. After about 5 miles, take the right fork (still Jackson County 12) toward Lake John. After 2.5 miles stay left on Jackson County 12, after 2 more miles stay to the right, then continue an additional 2 miles. At the "T" in the road turn left on Jackson County 16. From this point on, the roads are all-weather dirt roads that are rough in a few spots but do not require a four-wheel-drive vehicle. Pass through the Lone Pine Ranch and enter the Routt National Forest (Road 640) 5 miles from the T. The Grizzly-Helena Trail (#1126) intersects Lone Pine Road in two places. The trailhead (**Point A**) for the section of the Grizzly-Helena Trail that leads north to Bear Lakes is on the right (north) side of the road, 1.3 miles past the National Forest boundary. Several campsites are available along Lone Pine Road after it enters the forest and at the Lake Katherine trailhead at the end of the road.

Follow the Grizzly-Helena Trail north 1.5 miles to an intersection with the Bear Lakes/Ute Pass Trail (#1128) (**Point B**). Turn left onto Trail #1128 and immediately enter the Mount Zirkel Wilderness. About ½-mile past the turnoff the trail passes two rundown cabins. Just beyond the cabin ruins a rusty ore cart lies at the base of old mine tailings (**Point C**). The shaft of the Bear Creek Mine, still supported by its original timbers, lies at the top of the tailings, several hundred feet above the trail. Take time to climb up and peer into the mine, but do not enter it (for your safety, you should never enter old mines).

After a long, gradual climb, the trail levels out 2.5 miles beyond the mine. Follow the rock cairns through this flat section. At the far end of the level stretch the main trail switchbacks steeply up the side of a hill (**Point D**). The spur trail to Bear Lakes heads faintly downhill through an open grassy area on the left just before the main trail reaches the base of the hill. Although the first 200 feet of the Bear Lakes Trail is indistinct, the trail quickly becomes well defined. A large rock cairn marks the area where the Bear Lakes Trail enters the trees. The trail fades again in the wet meadows on the way to the lakes but is easy to relocate on the far side of these meadows. About ¾-mile from the turnoff, Upper Bear Lake (**Point E**) peeks through the trees to the right. The main trail continues

The entrance to the Bear Creek Mine. It is not safe to enter abandoned mines.

Looking east across Upper Bear Lake.

downhill and eventually winds around to the lakes. If you are fairly agile (and impatient), simply scramble down over the boulders to the northern shore of the upper lake.

Upper Bear Lake (10,343 feet, 10 acres) is a deep green alpine lake. The northern shore drops off sharply, and numerous large, angular boulders furnish perfect casting sites. Upper Bear Lake contains cutthroat to twelve inches, most of which seem to hide among crevices in submerged rocks along the shore. The western shore features a sandy beach and excellent views across the lake. There are no campsites at the upper lake. Southwest over a small ridge from the upper lake lies Lower Bear Lake (10,320 feet, 16 acres). The lower lake is surrounded by trees except for its rocky western shore. The cutthroat and brown trout present in Lower Bear Lake are a little longer and plumper than the fish in the upper lake. Several campsites are available in the trees between the two lakes.

To reach Ute Pass, stay on the main trail (#1128) at the Bear Lakes Trail turnoff (**Point D**). The main trail switchbacks uphill to an open level area where the remainder of the trail can be seen as a series of long switchbacks. Follow the switchbacks as they ascend the grassy slope to the top of Ute Pass (**Point F**). Ute Pass is wide and level, with trees obscuring many of the views to the north and west. The sweeping views back to the east and south of the Bear Creek valley and Bear Mountain are magnificent. Sun rays glinting off the deep green waters of Upper Bear Lake reveal its location to the southeast. Near the far (west) side of the flat section atop Ute Pass, small rock cairns mark the point where another trail leads to the northeast. This trail offers an alternate return route to the Grizzly-Helena Trail, around the northern side of Bear Mountain along Ute Creek. This loop trail intersects the Grizzly-Helena Trail (**Point G**) about 2.5 miles north of Bear Creek, so allow an extra one to two hours if you choose this option.

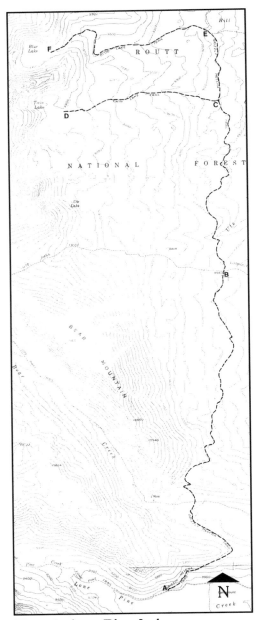

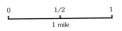

Twin Lakes, Blue Lake

0   1/2   1

1 mile

Twin Lakes, Blue Lake

Trailhead
>   Grizzly-Helena Trail (#1126) on Forest Service Road 640
>   (Lone Pine Road)

Starting elevation
>   8,870 feet

Ending elevation
>   Twin Lakes: 9,865 feet
>   Blue Lake: 9,815 feet

Distance (round trip)
>   Twin Lakes: 18 miles
>   Blue Lake: 20 miles

Time required (round trip)
>   Twin Lakes: 9 hours
>   Blue Lake: 10 hours

Rating
>   Twin Lakes: Moderate/Difficult
>   Blue Lake: Moderate/Difficult

Maps
>   7.5' Boettcher Lake
>   7.5' Pitchpine Mountain
>   Routt National Forest

Main attractions
>   Deep blue-green lakes; remote, rugged scenery; opportunity
>   to fish for lake trout.

Blue Lake and Twin Lakes are situated in beautiful, rugged country less than 2 miles from the eastern boundary of the Mount Zirkel Wilderness. Unfortunately, large areas of private land preclude easy access to this picturesque portion of the Wilderness. Although the Routt National Forest map shows several roads leading into the forest near the lakes along the eastern edge of the Wilderness, all of these roads are closed to the public. The only approach to these lakes involves a long trek (from either the north or the south) along the Grizzly-Helena Trail (#1126), which skirts the eastern edge of the Wilderness. Despite their distance from the trailhead, Blue and

87

Lower Twin Lake.

Twin Lakes are popular backpacking destinations. The route described here is from the south.

To reach the Grizzly-Helena trailhead, take Highway 14 east from Walden. About ¼-mile outside of town turn right (west) on Jackson County 12. After about 5 miles, take the right fork (still Jackson County 12) toward Lake John. After 2.5 miles, stay left on Jackson County 12, after 2 more miles stay to the right, then continue an additional 2 miles. At the "T" in the road turn left on Jackson County 16. From this point on, the roads are all-weather dirt roads that are rough in a few spots but do not require a four-wheel-drive vehicle. Pass through the Lone Pine Ranch and enter the Routt National Forest (Road 640) 5 miles from the T. The Grizzly-Helena Trail intersects Lone Pine Road in two spots. The trailhead (**Point A**) for the section of the Grizzly-Helena Trail that leads north to Twin and Blue lakes is on the right (north) side of the road, 1.3 miles past the National Forest boundary. Several camp-sites are available along Lone Pine Road after it enters the forest and at the Lake Katherine trailhead at the end of the road.

The first mile of the Grizzly-Helena Trail winds uphill through a dense stand of aspen. These trees turn the whole mountainside

Blue Lake nestled in its rugged basin.

fiery gold in September, making this first mile a beautiful late-season stroll. The trail descends to a crossing of Bear Creek 1.5 miles from the trailhead. Just beyond the creek continue straight past the turnoff to Bear Lakes and Ute Pass. Beyond the turnoff, pass through several open areas with sweeping views of the plains and distant mountains to the east. Do not be surprised to see cattle along the trail—the National Forest leases these lands for grazing. Four miles from the trailhead a road crosses the trail and ends at an old sign marking the boundary of the Mount Zirkel Wilderness. Bypass this old road and continue north on the Grizzly-Helena Trail to an intersection (**Point B**) 5 miles from the trailhead. The left fork at this intersection leads to Ute Pass; continue straight to reach Twin and Blue lakes. Two miles later the trail meets the turnoff to Twin Lakes alongside Lake Creek (**Point C**).

To reach Twin Lakes, follow the Twin Lakes Trail (#1174) as it gains 850 feet in 1.5 miles before arriving at the lakes (**Point D**). Twin Lakes (9,865 feet) lie in rugged, rocky terrain. The larger lake (23 acres) features a waterfall cascading down its steep and rocky western shore. The eastern and southern shores are open and strewn with boulders. This lake contains both brook trout and lake trout. Lake trout are difficult to catch, usually retreating to deeper water during summer. A small forested ridge separates the two lakes and offers the best campsites. The smaller lake offers excellent fishing for brook trout to twelve inches.

To reach Blue Lake, continue straight past the Twin Lakes turnoff, following the Grizzly-Helena Trail an additional mile to the Blue Lake Trail turnoff (**Point E**). The Blue Lake Trail (#1179) follows alongside Hill Creek before dropping down to Blue Lake (**Point F**) 1.7 miles from the turnoff.

The beautiful blue-green waters of Blue Lake (9,815 feet, 21 acres) are enclosed on three sides by sheer rock walls. Blue Lake is very deep, with good fishing for brook, rainbow, and lake trout. There are a few campsites above the lake along the creek to the east. A small stream tumbling down the southwestern shore of the lake is the outlet from Peggy Lake, which lies 1,300 feet and 1 mile above Blue Lake.

It is also possible to reach Blue Lake from Twin Lakes by hiking north from Twin Lakes over the gentler eastern portion of the ridge that separates the two basins. This route requires a compass and some bushwhacking, but the distance between the lakes is reduced to about ½-mile.

Rainbow Lakes

Trailhead
> *Rainbow Lakes Trailhead (#1130)*

Starting elevation
> *8,760 feet*

Ending elevation
> *9,854 feet*

Distance (round trip)
> *7 miles*

Time required (round trip)
> *3.5 hours*

Rating
> *Easy/Moderate*

Maps
> *7.5' Pitchpine Mountain*
> *7.5' Mount Ethel*
> *Routt National Forest*

Main attractions
> *Shady, fairly short hike to the largest lake in the Mount Zirkel Wilderness; excellent views of Mount Ethel; good backcountry camping.*

The deep blue waters of Rainbow Lakes draw large numbers of hikers every summer. This is one of the most popular trailheads on the east side of the Mount Zirkel Wilderness and is often crowded, especially on the July 4 and Labor Day weekends. However, the vast size of Rainbow Lake makes it fairly easy for those seeking solitude to find it. The trail to Rainbow Lake is fairly short and not too steep, making this an excellent hike for those looking for a quick escape into the mountains.

To reach the Rainbow Lakes trailhead, take Highway 14 east from Walden. About ¼-mile outside of town turn right (west) on Jackson County 12. After about 5 miles, stay to the left; the road becomes Jackson County Road 18. Follow County Road 18 approximately 4.5 miles until it intersects Jackson County Road 5. The pavement ends at this point and the road becomes an all-weather

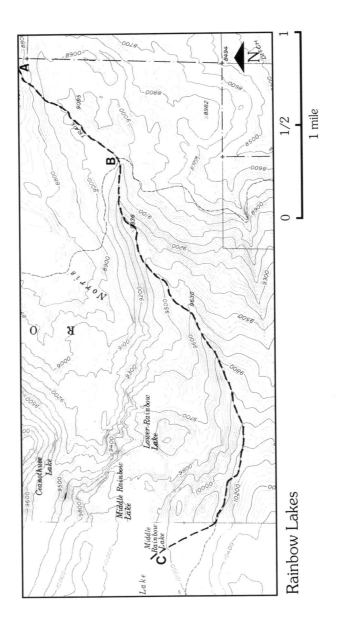

Rainbow Lakes

Ninety-six-acre Rainbow Lake is the largest lake in the Mount Zirkel Wilderness.

dirt road. At the "T" in the road turn left on County Road 5 and follow it for another 1.8 miles. At this point, County Road 5 turns left; continue straight ahead on Jackson County Road 22. Follow County Road 22 for 7.2 miles to the Routt National Forest boundary and another $\frac{1}{10}$-mile, where it dead-ends at the Rainbow Lakes trailhead (**Point A**). The road deteriorates somewhat as it approaches the National Forest boundary but is still easily passable by two-wheel-drive vehicles. There are few spots (maybe ten) that could be used as campsites at the Rainbow Lakes trailhead; if you plan to camp at the trailhead the night before your hike, get there early, especially on weekends.

The Rainbow Lakes Trail (#1130) begins in a mixed forest of aspen, lodgepole pine, spruce, and fir. Norris Creek, which drains out of Rainbow Lake, forms the valley to the right (north) of the trail. The trail intersects the Grizzly-Helena Trail (#1126) (**Point B**) just over $\frac{1}{2}$-mile from the trailhead. Continue straight on the Rainbow Lakes Trail, following a long ridgeline. Note the distinct difference in the forest types on the opposite sides of the ridge. The sunny south-facing slope is dominated by aspen, whereas the cooler north slope is mostly spruce and fir. Just over 2 miles from the trailhead the trail levels out and continues to head west under the welcome shade of large spruce and fir. The trail drops alongside Middle Rainbow Lake 3.5 miles from the trailhead. A few hundred feet beyond Middle Rainbow Lake lies Rainbow Lake (**Point C**).

Rainbow Lake (9,854 feet, 96 acres) is the largest lake in the Mount Zirkel Wilderness. Its impressive size, beautiful setting, easy access, and proximity to other destinations combine to make it a very popular destination. The sheer eastern flank of Mount Ethel, which usually retains snow year-round, is visible beyond the western shore of the lake and provides an impressive backdrop for photographs. Backpackers will find existing campsites scattered among the trees on the north and east sides of the lake. Many campsites are showing signs of overuse and some areas have been closed to allow vegetation to recover. Day hikers can spend hours relaxing along the shore of the lake and try to catch rainbow and cutthroat trout that lurk in the deep blue waters. Both Lower and Middle Rainbow lakes also contain rainbow and cutthroat trout.

The Rainbow Lakes Trail continues west past Rainbow Lake to Slide Lake, Upper Slide Lake, and the Roxy Ann Lake Trail before intersecting the Wyoming Trail (#1101) at the Continental Divide.

For hikers skilled at using a map and compass, another potential day hike destination is Ceanothuse Lake, which lies over the ridge to the north of Middle Rainbow Lake. There is no established trail to Ceanothuse Lake, but hikers can bushwhack into this small lake, which offers excellent fishing for cutthroat trout to fifteen inches.

Slide Lakes

Trailhead
> *Rainbow Lakes Trailhead (#1130)*

Starting elevation
> *8,760 feet*

Ending elevation
> *Slide Lake: 10,527 feet*
> *Upper Slide Lake: 10,760 feet*

Distance (round trip)
> *14.5 miles*

Time required (round trip)
> *7 hours*

Rating
> *Moderate*

Maps
> *7.5' Pitchpine Mountain*
> *7.5' Mount Ethel*
> *Routt National Forest*

Main attractions
> *Good backcountry camping at two of the prettiest lakes in the Mount Zirkel Wilderness; close to other lakes, peaks, and the Continental Divide; excellent fishing for plump cutthroat trout.*

Slide Lake and Upper Slide Lake are the upper set of lakes that lie on the eastern side of the Continental Divide along the Rainbow Lakes Trail (#1130). Slide Lakes are tucked into a rugged basin about 2 miles above the much larger and more crowded Rainbow Lakes. At just over 7 miles by trail (one way), the trip to Slide Lakes is a lengthy day hike. Slide Lakes offer excellent backcountry camping featuring beautiful scenery, excellent fishing, and a wide range of nearby destinations to visit. From Slide Lakes, potential day-hike destinations include Roxy Ann Lake, Lost Ranger Peak, the Dome, Pristine Lake, and Mount Ethel. Descriptions of these hikes are included in this guide.

To reach the Rainbow Lakes trailhead, take Highway 14 east from Walden. About ¼-mile outside of town turn right (west) on

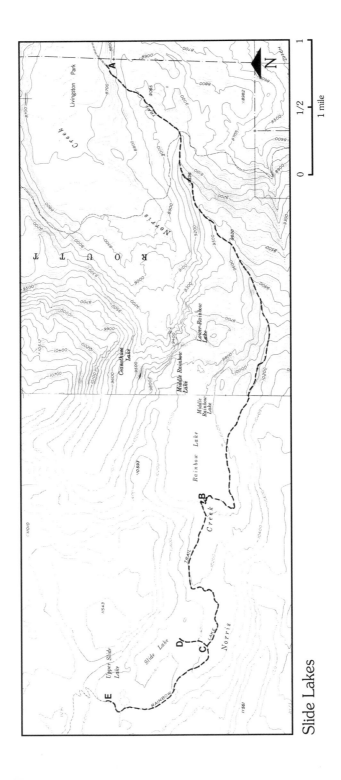

Slide Lakes

Slide Lake, as seen from the ridge below Upper Slide Lake.

Jackson County Road 12. After about 5 miles, stay to the left; the road becomes Jackson County Road 18. Follow County Road 18 approximately 4.5 miles until it intersects Jackson County Road 5. The pavement ends at this point and the road becomes an all-weather dirt road. At the T in the road turn left on County Road 5 and follow it for another 1.8 miles. At this point, County Road 5 turns left; continue straight ahead on Jackson County Road 22. Follow County Road 22 for 7.2 miles to the Routt National Forest boundary and another ⅒-mile, where it dead-ends at the Rainbow Lakes trailhead (**Point A**). The road deteriorates somewhat as it approaches the National Forest boundary but is still easily passable by two-wheel-drive vehicles. There are few spots (maybe ten) that could be used as campsites near the Rainbow Lakes Trailhead; if you plan to camp at the trailhead the night before your hike, get there early, especially on weekends.

To reach Slide Lakes, follow the hike narration to Rainbow Lakes on page 91. From Rainbow Lake, follow the trail along the south side of the lake for 1.25 miles. After reaching the far (west) side of Rainbow Lake, cross the inlet stream and head uphill alongside a waterfall (**Point B**). After a short, steep climb, the trail reaches the top of a ridge and enters a wet meadow. Continue through a series of meadows where the rugged east face of Mount Ethel provides a majestic backdrop for photos.

The trail crosses over the outlet stream from Slide Lake (**Point C**) 1.5 miles after leaving the western shore of Rainbow Lake. The outlet stream comes down the hillside on the right (north) side of the trail and enters the slowly moving larger stream to the left of the trail. The easiest route to Slide Lake turns right here and follows the outlet stream as it cascades over bedrock for ¼-mile to the lower (eastern) end of Slide Lake (**Point D**). Note that this "shortcut" to Slide Lake is not marked by a sign and lacks a distinct trail along the outlet stream.

If you choose not to take the shortcut (or simply miss it), the main trail crosses the outlet stream and continues to gain elevation. The trail stays about ¼-mile southwest of Slide Lake, and the lake remains out of sight. About 1.25 miles after crossing the outlet stream the trail passes the western shore of Upper Slide Lake (10,760 feet, 9 acres) (**Point E**). Head downhill along the southwest shore of Upper Slide Lake to reach Slide Lake.

Slide Lake (10,527 feet, 27 acres) is one of the most scenic lakes in the Mount Zirkel Wilderness. The lake is named for its northeast shore, which is composed of large angular rocks that lie at the base of a steep rock face. These rocks appear to have "slid" into the lake. The views from this rocky northeast shore across the deep blue-green water, with Mount Ethel towering in the background, are spectacular. Slide Lake is a popular backcountry camping area; the best campsites are in the trees on the south and east sides of the lake. Both Slide lakes offer good fishing. Upper Slide Lake features brook and cutthroat trout. Slide Lake offers excellent fishing for plump cutthroat trout to fifteen inches. The deep waters along Slide Lake's rocky northeast shore harbor the most fish and provide the best action.

For those who wish to continue to other destinations, the Rainbow Lakes Trail continues beyond Upper Slide Lake to the Roxy Ann Lake Trail (#1179) turnoff before intersecting the Wyoming Trail (#1101) at the Continental Divide.

Roxy Ann Lake

Trailhead
> *Rainbow Lakes Trailhead (#1130)*

Starting elevation
> *8,760 feet*

Ending elevation
> *10,204 feet*

Distance (round trip)
> *19 miles*

Time required (round trip)
> *9.5 hours*

Rating
> *Difficult*

Maps
> *7.5′ Pitchpine Mountain*
> *7.5′ Mount Ethel*
> *Routt National Forest*

Main attractions
> *Excellent fishing; beautiful backcountry camping; sandy beach; solitude.*

Although perched in a basin only 3 straight-line miles from the Wilderness boundary, Roxy Ann Lake is surprisingly difficult to reach. The shortest approach, via Rainbow and Slide lakes, is described below, but even this route involves a long hike with numerous changes in elevation. The lake is also accessible from the Wyoming Trail (#1101) between Mount Ethel and Lost Ranger Peak. Regardless of approach, an overnight trip is required to reach Roxy Ann Lake. Its combination of deep blue-green water, sandy shoreline, and excellent fishing for cutthroat trout make it an ideal backpacking destination.

To reach the Rainbow Lakes trailhead, take Highway 14 east from Walden. About ¼-mile outside of town, turn right (west) on Jackson County Road 12. After about 5 miles, stay to the left; the road becomes Jackson County Road 18. Follow County Road 18 approximately 4.5 miles until it intersects Jackson County Road 5.

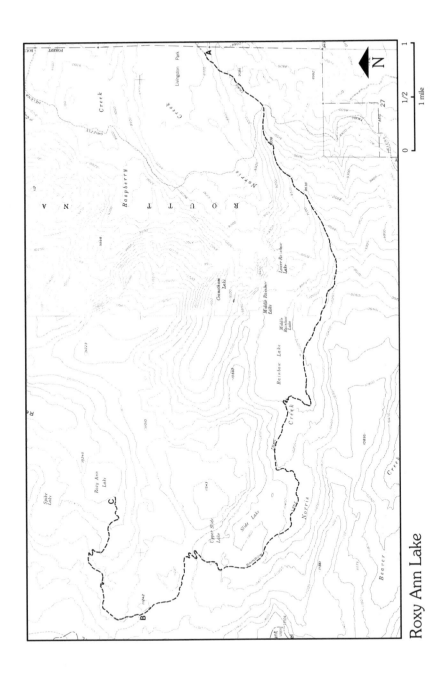

Roxy Ann Lake

Beautiful Roxy Ann Lake is an ideal destination for backpackers.

The pavement ends and the road becomes an all-weather dirt road. At the "T" in the road turn left on County Road 5 and follow it for another 1.8 miles. At this point County Road 5 turns left; continue straight ahead on Jackson County Road 22. Follow County Road 22 for 7.2 miles to the Routt National Forest boundary and continue another 1/10-mile, where the road dead-ends at the Rainbow Lakes trailhead (**Point A**). The road deteriorates somewhat as it approaches the National Forest boundary but is still easily passable by two-wheel-drive vehicles. There are few spots (maybe ten) that could be used as campsites at the Rainbow Lakes trailhead; if you want to camp at the trailhead the night before your hike, plan to arrive early.

To reach Roxy Ann Lake, follow the hike narration to Upper Slide Lake on page 95. From Upper Slide Lake, the Rainbow Lakes Trail winds uphill through open, rocky countryside for ¾-mile to the turnoff to Roxy Ann Lake (**Point B**). Turn right and follow the sandy but distinct Roxy Ann Lake Trail (#1179) as it descends beneath rugged rock outcrops. Snowfields persist at the base of these outcrops year-round. Pass through several wet meadows that display colorful wildflowers even late in the summer. Rock cairns and signposts mark the route when the trail fades. Three-quarters of a mile from the turnoff, Roxy Ann Lake finally comes into view far below. The trail continues to descend toward the lake, becoming slippery and rough in spots. There are several trails that branch away from the main trail and head down to the lake; try to stay on the most distinct one. All trails converge at the western edge of the lake, so it is impossible to lose your way. About ¼-mile above the lake, cross the inlet stream and begin the final descent. About 1.75 miles after leaving the Rainbow Lakes Trail you will arrive at Roxy Ann Lake (**Point C**).

Roxy Ann Lake (10,204 feet, 63 acres) is the second largest lake in the Mount Zirkel Wilderness. Forest surrounds the lake on all sides, but the trees do not reach to the water's edge in most areas. The western shore is very sandy with steep drop-offs into deep blue water—an ideal place for a swim on warm days. The northern shore features a series of rock outcrops that provide excellent vantage points for peering into the clear deep water to watch cutthroat trout cruising along the base of the rocky cliffs. The trout reach good size in Roxy Ann Lake, up to twenty inches long and over two pounds. However, they are surprisingly wary and hard to catch, considering the remoteness of the lake. Campsites are available along the western shore where the trail meets the lake.

Roxy Ann Lake can also be reached from the Wyoming Trail (#1101) along the Continental Divide. The lake is visible from the Continental Divide and beckons many hikers with its size and beauty. A sign on the Wyoming Trail between Mount Ethel and Lost Ranger Peak marks the Rainbow Lakes Trail (#1130) toward Roxy Ann Lake, Slide Lakes, and Rainbow Lakes. Trail #1130 heads east from the divide ½-mile to the Roxy Ann Lake Trail turnoff.

Newcomb Park

Trailhead
> *Newcomb Creek Trailhead (#1132)*

Starting elevation
> *8,740 feet*

Ending elevation
> *8,800 feet*

Distance (round trip)
> *4 miles*

Time required (round trip)
> *2 hours*

Rating
> *Easy*

Maps
> *7.5' Teal Lake*
> *7.5' Buffalo Pass*
> *Routt National Forest*

Main attractions
> *A short, level hike through a series of mountain meadows; ample opportunities for wildlife viewing; a good hike for families with young children.*

With no particular ending destination, the Newcomb Creek Trail (#1132) is ideal for those seeking an easy walk in the Wilderness or leisurely fishing in Newcomb Creek. The following narration ends 2 miles from the trailhead, where the trail crosses Newcomb Creek but before it begins to gain elevation. The hike can be shortened if desired or lengthened by continuing to Round Mountain Lake. Since the majority of time spent on this trail is in open meadows, be sure to bring plenty of water (and sunscreen) on warm, sunny days.

To reach the trailhead, take Highway 14 west out of Walden to Hebron. Turn right (west) at Hebron and continue on Jackson County Road 24 for 11.2 miles to the Grizzly Campground. Drive just past the campground and turn right on Forest Service Road 615. Follow Road 615 approximately 4 miles, past Tiago Lake and Teal Lake, to a sign on the left side of the road marking the Newcomb

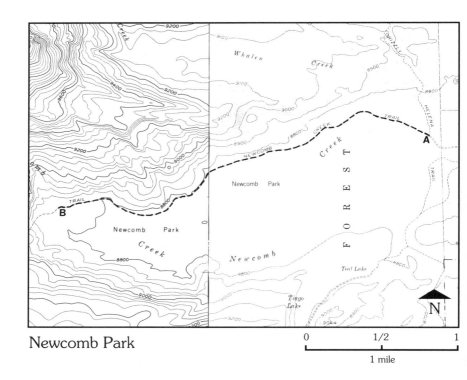

Newcomb Park

0   1/2   1

1 mile

Trail meandering through Newcomb Park.

Creek trailhead. Turn left at the sign and drive ¼-mile to the trailhead (**Point A**). There are three or four good sites for camping at the trailhead—but no water is available, so bring plenty if you plan to camp here. We suggest camping at nearby Teal Lake Campground or Grizzly Campground.

The trail into Newcomb Park begins at the Mount Zirkel Wilderness sign. Cross a stream just beyond the sign and enter a meadow full of willows. Spruce and fir surround the meadow to the south and north. Newcomb Creek flows lazily off to the left about twenty-five feet from the trail. The meadows are abundant with wildflowers, as well as many species of birds, snakes, frogs, small mammals, with an occasional deer. About 1.25 miles from the trailhead, climb over a small hill and immediately emerge into another large meadow. This meadow, unlike the first, is composed mostly of grasses, with few willows. Straight ahead to the west is a wonderful view of Round Mountain. Cross the meadow and pass through a brief forested area before entering yet another meadow. The trail is now overgrown by short grasses but still easy to follow. Just over 1.75 miles from the trailhead pass through more aspen and continue into an enormous meadow with a small pond on its south side. Two miles from the trailhead the trail crosses Newcomb Creek (**Point B**) and begins to climb steeply.

We recommend that you end your Newcomb Park hike at the Newcomb Creek crossing unless you wish to hike the remaining 2.5 miles to Round Mountain Lake. The hike to Round Mountain Lake is short but steep, gaining 1,000 feet in elevation between the Newcomb Creek crossing (**Point B**) and Round Mountain Lake. An alternate route to Round Mountain Lake is described in the next section.

Destinations in the Central Mount Zirkel Wilderness

The rugged and remote interior of the Mount Zirkel Wilderness offers unparalleled opportunities for backpackers and anglers. Since the majority of destinations in this section are too distant to reach easily in a single day, we recommend backpacking into a back-country lake, setting up a base camp, and spending several days exploring the surrounding lakes and peaks. Another way to explore the central section of the Wilderness is to backpack along the Continental Divide on the Wyoming Trail, descending each night to any of the numerous lakes nestled along the divide to set up camp.

Notable destinations in this part of the Wilderness include Mount Ethel, Lost Ranger Peak, and the Dome. All of these summits afford spectacular views from the heart of the Wilderness. Those seeking good fishing at beautiful alpine lakes should shoulder a backpack and head for Lake Elbert, Luna Lake, or Lake Margaret.

Most destinations in the central Mount Zirkel Wilderness can be reached from the east, west, or south. Because we cannot predict the location of every hiker's base camp, directions to most of the destinations in this section begin at the Wyoming Trail at Buffalo Pass. As a result, most of the round-trip distances and times given in the hike headings represent the maximum possible hiking distance.

Directions to Buffalo Pass

The trailhead for most destinations in this section is the Wyoming Trail, located on Forest Service Road 60 near the summit of Buffalo Pass. Forest Service Road 60 can be reached from the west via Steamboat Springs or from the east via Walden.

To get to the trailhead from Steamboat Springs, take Highway 40 into downtown Steamboat Springs. Turn right (north) onto 7th Street. After ⅓-mile, take another right onto Missouri Avenue. After another ⅓-mile, Missouri Avenue turns sharply left and becomes North Park Road. Two and a half miles from the intersection of Highway 40 and 7th Street, turn right onto Routt County Road 38. Within ¼-mile the road becomes an all-weather dirt road. County Road 38 enters the Routt National Forest and becomes Forest Service Road 60. Road 60 is rough and bouncy for most of its 8 miles to Buffalo Pass but does not require four-wheel-drive. The Wyoming Trail (#1101) leaves from the left (north) side of Road 60 just before the road reaches Buffalo Pass.

From Walden, take Highway 14 west to Hebron. Turn right (west) at Hebron and continue on Jackson County Road 24 for 11.2 miles until you reach the Grizzly Campground. Drive past the campground, continuing straight on to Forest Service Road 60. Road 60 is rough and rocky; four-wheel-drive is recommended for clearing rocks, but the road is passable with two-wheel-drive vehicles. Road 60 reaches the summit of Buffalo Pass 8.5 miles beyond the Grizzly Campground. The Wyoming Trail (#1101) leaves from the right (north) side of Road 60 just beyond the pass.

Round Mountain Lake

Trailhead
   Wyoming Trail (#1101) at Buffalo Pass
Starting elevation
   10,300 feet
Ending elevation
   9,860 feet
Distance (round trip)
   9 miles
Time required (round trip)
   5 hours
Rating
   Easy/Moderate
Maps
   7.5′ Buffalo Pass
   Routt National Forest
Main attractions
   Hike along the Continental Divide to a seldom-visited lake; good fishing for brook trout.

Round Mountain Lake receives little visitation and is an excellent backcountry choice for those seeking solitude. The first 2 miles of the hike follow the Wyoming Trail (#1101) as it winds north near the Continental Divide through spectacular wildflowers. A trip to Round Mountain Lake also offers a benefit rarely found in Colorado hiking—a trail that actually loses elevation between the trailhead and the destination. This hike is recommended for experienced hikers only, because after hikers leave the Wyoming Trail 2 miles from the trailhead, there are no signs and only a faint trail to guide them to the lake.

Follow the directions to Buffalo Pass given on page 107. From the Wyoming Trail trailhead (**Point A**), the trail heads steadily uphill to the north. Before this area received wilderness designation in 1964, a jeep road led all the way to Luna Lake, and the trail still follows the old road most of the way. Amidst colorful Indian paintbrush and purple lupines, the trail quickly enters the Mount Zirkel

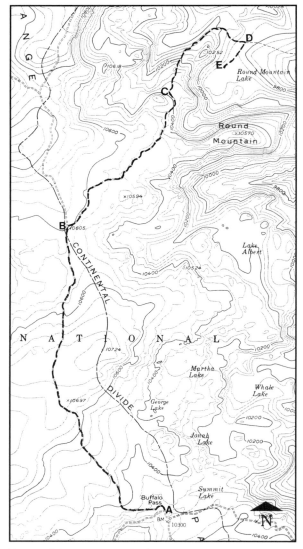

Round Mountain Lake

0   1/2   1

1 mile

Round Mountain Lake, as seen from the ridge south of the Newcomb Creek Trail.

Wilderness. One mile from the trailhead the trail levels out and enters a meadow scattered with yellow glacier lilies and yellow paintbrush. At the far end of the meadow the trail crests, revealing impressive views to the north of Mount Ethel, which retains its mantle of snow well into July.

Exactly 2 miles from the trailhead a sign marks the Newcomb Creek Trail (#1132) on the right (**Point B**). Turn right (east) and follow the rock cairns that mark the Newcomb Creek Trail as it fades in and out. Trails that are not heavily used (such as the Newcomb Creek Trail) rapidly become indistinct in wet grassy stretches, making it critical to watch carefully for the rock cairns that guide the way until the trail becomes clear again. After leaving the meadow and entering scattered patches of spruce and fir, the trail beomes a single track. About 1.2 miles from the turnoff onto the Newcomb Creek Trail, pass to the left of a small pond (**Point C**). About ½-mile beyond the pond, superb views to the northwest reveal the jagged ridgeline that forms the eastern perimeter of the Continental Divide. Once the trail levels out, there are several spots where it is possible to climb several hundred feet up to the ridge south (right) of the trail for views of Round Mountain Lake nestled far below in the trees. To reach the lake, continue on the main trail through a short section where the trail again fades. Watch carefully for the Round Mountain Lake Trail turnoff (**Point D**). The turnoff is not marked by a sign, but several blazes on the east side of a spruce tree mark the point where the well-defined Round Mountain Lake Trail leaves the Newcomb Creek Trail and angles sharply back to the right (southwest). Follow the Round Mountain Lake Trail for ⅓-mile until it ends at the northern shore of Round Mountain Lake (**Point E**).

Round Mountain Lake (9,860 feet, 10 acres) is surrounded by trees except for a grassy slope sprinkled with large boulders on its western shore. There are several campsites scattered around the lake, especially along the northern shore. Round Mountain Lake is teeming with twelve-inch brook trout and can provide an afternoon of productive fishing before you return to the trailhead via the same route.

Those who wish to hike farther can follow the Newcomb Creek Trail, which continues east for 5 miles until it reaches its trailhead along Forest Service Road 615 on the eastern edge of the Mount Zirkel Wilderness.

Porcupine Lake

Trailhead
> *Wyoming Trail (#1101) at Buffalo Pass*

Starting elevation
> *10,300 feet*

Ending elevation
> *10,480 feet*

Distance (round trip)
> *14 miles*

Time required (round trip)
> *8 hours*

Rating
> *Moderate/Difficult*

Maps
> *7.5' Buffalo Pass*
> *Routt National Forest*

Main attractions
> *Clear green water and sandy bottom; ideal backcountry swimming hole.*

Porcupine Lake is a small lake that sits just south of Lake Elbert. A primitive trail (#1202) leading from the Wyoming Trail (#1101) to Lake Elbert passes alongside Porcupine Lake, though few people take this route. Although it's difficult to follow in spots, Trail #1202 passes through a beautiful alpine meadow between Porcupine Lake and Lake Elbert and offers a worthwhile alternate route between Buffalo Pass and the interior of the Mount Zirkel Wilderness.

Follow the directions to Buffalo Pass given on page 107. Begin the hike to Porcupine Lake at the Wyoming Trail trailhead (**Point A**). Because there is virtually no place to get water on the way to Porcupine Lake, be sure to bring plenty with you. The first 5 miles of the hike to Porcupine Lake follow the Wyoming Trail as it meanders along the Continental Divide. (Further description of this route is provided in the Luna Lake hike narration, on page 117.) The Wyoming Trail follows the old road to Luna Lake for nearly 5 miles. At this point the trail deviates from the old road and begins

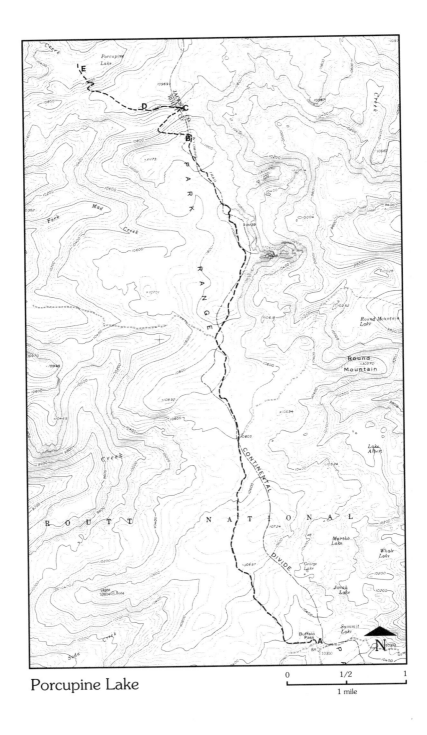

Porcupine Lake

0   1/2   1

1 mile

The inviting green waters of Porcupine Lake tempt hikers to dive in on hot, sunny days.

descending a long switchback (**Point B**). While descending the switchback, look down into the valley for a glimpse of the Porcupine Lake Trail (#1202) heading west far below. Just before the Wyoming Trail turns sharply to the right near the valley bottom, the faint Porcupine Lake Trail (**Point C**) can be seen to the left. The trail is not signed, but an old red blaze on a large spruce tree marks the point where it cuts between the trees and heads west. Slowly wind uphill on the Porcupine Lake Trail above the low point of the valley. The trail levels out and enters a long, grassy meadow scattered with large rocks (**Point D**). Watch for small cairns to guide the way as the now-indistinct trail proceeds down the center of the meadow for the next ½-mile. At the far end of the meadow, just before it drops off sharply, two small rock cairns mark the point where the trail turns right and cuts downhill through an opening in the trees. After descending a steep grassy slope and passing through a final level section, Porcupine Lake (**Point E**) comes into view in the valley below.

Porcupine Lake (10,480 feet, 4 acres) sits in a small grassy basin. Unlike most lakes in the wilderness, Porcupine Lake has no trees near the shoreline. The water is clear and green and becomes quite deep near the middle of the lake. The soft sandy shores and inviting green water tempt weary hikers to wade or swim. In fact, on hot summer days a dip in the cold water of Porcupine Lake is amazingly refreshing. Although occasionally stocked with fish, the lake is prone to winterkill and is not recommended to anglers.

From Porcupine Lake, the trail continues north through a beautiful alpine valley before arriving at Lake Elbert, 1 mile away.

Luna Lake, Lake Elbert

Trailhead
> *Wyoming Trail (#1101) at Buffalo Pass*

Starting elevation
> *10,300 feet*

Ending elevation
> *Luna Lake: 10,482 feet*
> *Lake Elbert: 10,800 feet*

Distance (round trip)
> *Luna Lake: 18 miles*
> *Lake Elbert: 16 miles*

Time required (round trip)
> *Luna Lake: 9 hours*
> *Lake Elbert: 8 hours*

Rating
> *Moderate/Difficult*

Maps
> *7.5' Buffalo Pass*
> *7.5' Mount Ethel*
> *Routt National Forest*

Main attractions
> *Beautiful alpine lakes; excellent base camp for exploring central portion of the Mount Zirkel Wilderness; good backcountry campsites.*

Luna Lake and Lake Elbert lie along the western edge of the Continental Divide in the heart of the Mount Zirkel Wilderness. Unlike the narrow northern and southern portions of the Wilderness, the central section is quite wide. As a result, most destinations in this region are more than a day's walk from any trailhead. Both Luna Lake and Lake Elbert are ideal places to set up a base camp from which to explore the rugged and remote interior of the Mount Zirkel Wilderness.

Luna Lake was a popular destination in the 1950s and early 1960s. Prior to the creation of the Mount Zirkel Wilderness in 1964, a jeep road led from Buffalo Pass to Luna Lake. The trail to Luna

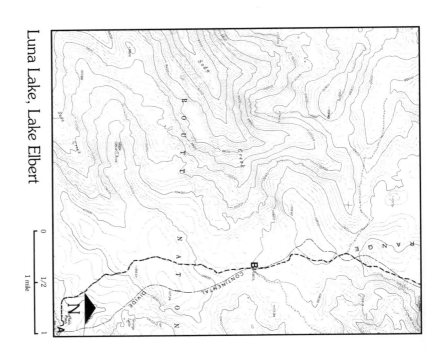

Luna Lake, Lake Elbert

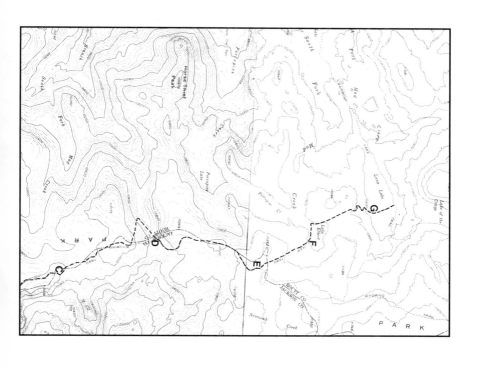

Descending from the Continental Divide to Lake Elbert.

Lake follows the tire tracks of the old road most of the way, but the considerable effort required to walk rather than ride those 9 miles has thinned the crowds at the lake to a trickle. Although the change in elevation between the trailhead and the lake is less than 200 feet, the trail to Luna Lake alternately gains and loses elevation many times along its course. The hike to Lake Elbert and Luna Lake can be accomplished by strong hikers as a long day hike; we recommend shouldering a backpack (or renting a llama or goat) for the trip.

Follow the directions to Buffalo Pass on page 107. From the Wyoming Trail trailhead (**Point A**), the trail heads steadily uphill to the north. Be sure to bring plenty of water with you, because there is virtually no place to replenish your supply before reaching Lake Elbert. Amidst colorful Indian paintbrush and purple lupines, the trail quickly enters the Mount Zirkel Wilderness. One mile from the trailhead the trail levels out and enters a meadow scattered with yellow glacier lilies and yellow paintbrush. At the far end of the meadow, a crest in the trail reveals impressive views along the Continental Divide of Mount Ethel, which retains its mantle of snow well into July. Exactly 2 miles from the trailhead a sign marks the Newcomb

Jay nearing the Continental Divide above Lake Elbert.

Creek Trail (#1132) (**Point B**) heading off to the right. Continue straight on the Wyoming Trail, climb a small ridge, and descend to a pond. Beyond the pond, climb steadily through a series of meadows for the next 2 miles to the Continental Divide, enjoying spectacular views to the east on the way. The point where the trail reaches the Continental Divide (**Point C**) is marked by a weathered wooden stake to the left of the trail and a brass U.S. Geological Survey marker embedded in a trailside rock. This spot marks not only the divide, but also the halfway point for the hike to Luna Lake.

Beyond the divide, the Wyoming Trail crosses large grassy meadows and open rock-strewn areas typical of this elevation. At the top of a long, gentle switchback, the trail deviates from the old road and begins to descend. The switchback eventually rejoins the old road (**Point D**) in the valley ½-mile below. After crossing the valley, begin to gradually climb uphill until you again reach the Continental Divide 2 miles past the base of the long switchback. This climb, while arduous, passes through beautiful sparsely treed meadows and provides splendid views back to the south. About 200 yards before reaching the Continental Divide a very faint fork

Luna Lake from the Crags Trail.

can be seen in the trail. At this point the Wyoming Trail turns right and continues north; stay to the left on the main, well-defined trail.

The Continental Divide (**Point E**) is marked by a sign indicating the trail to Lake Elbert, which comes into view 200 feet farther down the trail. If the weather is clear it is possible to see the large, rocky outcrop that rises behind Luna Lake and, farther off in the distance, the distinctive white-topped summit of Hahn's Peak. The trail leading down to Lake Elbert is faint in spots, especially as it crosses the wet meadow south of the lake. Stay on the trail as much as possible (to prevent further damage to the meadow) and aim for the southern shore of the lake near the outlet stream. Eight miles from the trailhead at Buffalo Pass the trail arrives at Lake Elbert (**Point F**).

Lake Elbert (10,800 feet, 11 acres) is a deep alpine lake situated near timberline. Its treeless shoreline provides excellent opportunities to fly-fish for cutthroat and rainbow trout to sixteen inches. Anglers fishing with lures should head for the cove on the eastern shore of the lake, where the water is very deep. The best campsites at Lake Elbert are near the southern shore. Unless you are completely exhausted, we recommend continuing to Luna Lake to set up camp.

The trail to Luna Lake passes Lake Elbert and climbs to a ridge between the lakes. Once at the ridge, cross through a short meadow and begin a very steep descent to Luna Lake. Follow the trail across the meadow on the eastern shore of Luna Lake. The trail reaches Luna Lake (**Point G**) 9 miles from the trailhead and 1 mile past Lake Elbert.

Luna Lake (10,482 feet, 38 acres) is one of the prettiest lakes in the Mount Zirkel Wilderness. It is a large, oval-shaped lake with a sandy beach along its eastern shore. A massive rock face rises impressively beyond the northern shore. The best campsites are hidden among the trees along the northern shore. Luna Lake offers excellent fishing for cutthroat trout to twenty inches. Because of its beautiful setting, central location, and excellent fishing, Luna Lake is one of our favorite backpacking destinations in the Wilderness. Day hikes from Luna Lake include Lake of the Crags, the Dome, Lost Ranger Peak, Roxy Ann Lake, Big Creek Lake, Mount Ethel, and the chain of lakes near Lake Margaret.

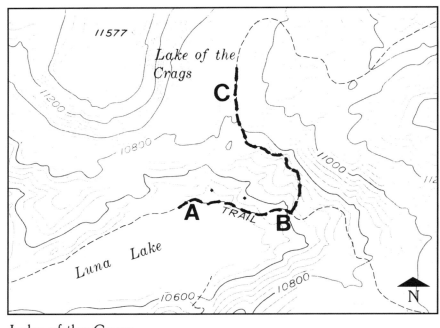

Lake of the Crags

Lake of the Crags

Trailhead
> *Crags Trail (#1182) from Luna Lake*

Starting elevation
> *10,482 feet*

Ending elevation
> *10,850 feet*

Distance (round trip)
> *1 mile (from Luna Lake)*

Time required (round trip)
> *30 minutes (from Luna Lake)*

Rating
> *Moderate*

Maps
> *7.5' Buffalo Pass*
> *7.5' Mount Ethel*
> *Routt National Forest*

Main attractions
> *Small lake nestled beneath a towering rock face; excellent stopover on a multiday hike.*

Like the other destinations discussed in this section, Lake of the Crags is located too far from a trailhead to be reached easily in one day. It lies to the north of the much larger Luna Lake, along the western edge of the Continental Divide in the interior of the Mount Zirkel Wilderness. Although not surrounded by crags, the lake is tucked against the base of a large rocky mountain that rises sharply to 11,577 feet. Its rugged setting furnishes superb photo opportunities, especially in the early morning when the sun illuminates the sheer western face behind the lake. The hike description begins from the northeast corner of Luna Lake.

Follow the directions to Luna Lake on page 117. The trail to Lake of the Crags begins along a stream flowing into the northeast corner of Luna Lake (**Point A**). Shortly after you leave Luna Lake, continue straight past a sign for the Crags Trail (#1182), where no trail is evident. Continue on the well-defined trail (#1168) for

Sunrise at Lake of the Crags.

another 300 feet to a second trail sign (**Point B**). Turn left at this
sign (toward CDT—Continental Divide Trail) and follow the rocky
but distinct Crags Trail uphill. About 200 feet beyond the sign,
bypass a dilapidated cabin to the left and continue to gain altitude
through sparse patches of spruce and fir. About ⁷⁄₁₀-mile above Luna
Lake, break out of the trees and enter an area of large, rounded
rock outcrops. A short detour to the left (west) reveals fine views of
Luna Lake, which appears to be surprisingly distant in its basin 350
feet below. Just beyond this rocky section the trail arrives at Lake of
the Crags (**Point C**).

Lake of the Crags (10,850 feet, 6 acres) lies beneath a towering rock face that rises dramatically above its western shore. The
shoreline is mostly open, with campsites on the eastern and
southern shores. A small island sits near the center of the lake.
Brightly colored cutthroat trout can be seen dimpling the glasslike
surface of the lake on calm days.

Beyond Lake of the Crags, the Crags Trail continues to climb
slowly through alpine tundra. About 1 mile above Lake of the
Crags, the trail intersects the Wyoming Trail (#1101) on the
Continental Divide.

Big Creek Lake

Trailhead
> Big Creek Lake Trail (#1184) from Luna Lake

Starting elevation
> 10,482 feet

Ending elevation
> 10,620 feet

Distance (round trip)
> 3.5 miles (from Luna Lake)

Time required (round trip)
> 2 hours (from Luna Lake)

Rating
> Easy

Maps
> 7.5′ Buffalo Pass
> 7.5′ Mount Ethel
> Routt National Forest

Main attractions
> Easy day hike from Luna Lake; good fishing for cutthroat trout.

Big Creek Lake lies in the west-central section of the Mount Zirkel Wilderness, about 2 miles northwest of Luna Lake. Access to this basin involves an overnight hike either from the west via Swamp Park or the south via Buffalo Pass to Luna Lake, so plan on spending a few days exploring other lakes and the surrounding peaks in this part of the Wilderness. Do not confuse this Big Creek Lake with the much larger Big Creek Lakes, located near Seven Lakes just outside the northeast boundary of the Mount Zirkel Wilderness. The hike description below begins at Luna Lake.

To reach the Big Creek Lake trailhead, follow the directions to Luna Lake given on page 117. From Luna Lake (**Point A**), follow the Luna Lake Trail (#1168) west along the northern shore of the lake. The trail to Big Creek Lake (#1184) intersects the Luna Lake Trail just west of Luna Lake's outlet. A sign at the intersection (**Point B**) indicates the well-defined trail to Big Creek Lake. The trail to Big Creek Lake immediately heads downhill and continues downhill

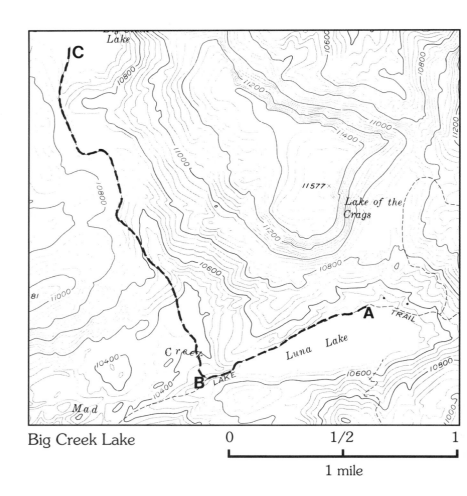

C

A

B

Lake

Lake of the Crags

11577 ×

Luna Lake

Creek

LAKE

Mad

TRAIL

Big Creek Lake

0   1/2   1

1 mile

Big Creek Lake.

for ¼-mile to a boulder-strewn meadow surrounding the Middle Fork of Mad Creek. Cross the Middle Fork and continue through the meadow. After leaving the meadow, climb uphill; two switchbacks complete the steep section of the trail. One mile from the intersection with the Luna Lake Trail, the Big Creek Lake Trail reaches the top of a ridge and enters a huge open area. The top of the ridge consists mostly of bedrock interspersed with grasses, which make the trail difficult to follow. Watch for rock cairns marking the best route. After reaching the northern edge of the ridge the trail disappears completely in the grassy meadow ahead. The meadow is surrounded by rock-covered ridges. Head straight across the meadow toward the low spot between the ridges surrounding the meadow to the north. A rock cairn is located in the low spot between the ridges. The trail can be found just to the right of the cairn, near the trees. Head downhill through spruce and fir trees until Big Creek Lake becomes visible. Continue another ¹⁄₁₀-mile down to the lake (**Point C**).

Big Creek Lake (10,620 feet, 8 acres) is nestled in a basin ringed on all sides by steep, rocky ridges. Plenty of campsites can be found along the south, east, and west shores. A grassy, boulder-laden meadow separates the lake from the surrounding high ridges. The water is shallow around the edges, but the middle of Big Creek Lake is a deep shade of blue. Because of its treeless shoreline, Big Creek Lake is an ideal place to fly-fish for ten- to twelve-inch cutthroat trout.

Mirror Lake, Lake Margaret, Lake Edward, Snowstorm Lake, Fishhawk Lake

Trailhead
> *Luna Lake Trail (#1168) from Luna Lake*

Starting elevation
> *10,482 feet*

Ending elevation
> *Mirror Lake: 10,040 feet*
> *Lake Margaret: 9,987 feet*
> *Lake Edward: 9,867 feet*
> *Snowstorm Lake: 9,747 feet*
> *Fishhawk Lake: 9,700 feet*

Distance (round trip)
> *4 to 7 miles (from Luna Lake)*

Time required (round trip)
> *2 to 4 hours (from Luna Lake)*

Rating
> *Moderate/Difficult*

Maps
> *7.5' Buffalo Pass*
> *7.5' Mount Ethel*
> *7.5' Floyd Peak*
> *Routt National Forest*

Main attractions
> *Excellent fishing in a lovely chain of natural lakes; good backcountry campsites; uncrowded.*

Lying within 1.5 miles of one another in the west-central Mount Zirkel Wilderness, these lakes offer unsurpassed opportunities for solitude and backcountry camping. Access to this chain of lakes involves an overnight hike either from Swamp Park to the west or from Buffalo Pass via Luna Lake, so plan on spending a few days exploring these lakes and others nestled among the surrounding peaks. All five lakes offer good fishing, although the biggest fish lurk

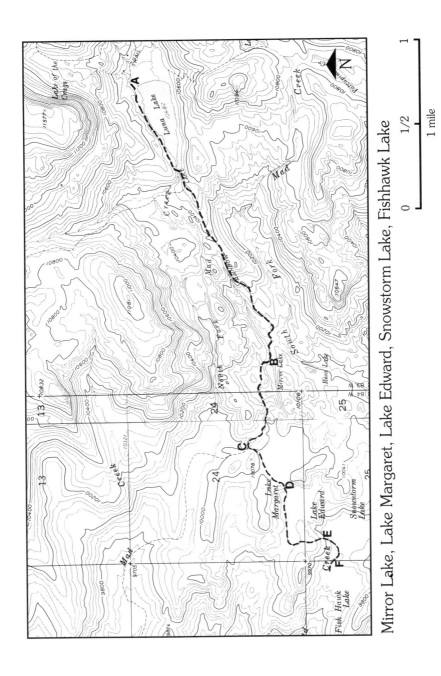

Mirror Lake, Lake Margaret, Lake Edward, Snowstorm Lake, Fishhawk Lake

Mirror Lake.

in the two largest lakes, Edward and Margaret. With five lakes lying in close proximity to one another, backcountry campsites are plentiful and it is easy to find a place to yourself.

To reach these lakes, follow the directions to Luna Lake on page 117. From Luna Lake (**Point A**), follow the Luna Lake Trail (#1168) west along the northern shore of the lake. Beyond the western edge of Luna Lake the trail winds uphill into spruce and fir. Continue heading west on the Luna Lake Trail past the sign indicating the trail to Big Creek Lake. After climbing gently for another ¼-mile, the trail levels out and meanders through sparse trees interspersed with meadows. One and three-quarter miles beyond Luna Lake, Mirror Lake comes into view at the far end of a meadow. The trail reaches Mirror Lake (**Point B**) ¼-mile farther.

Mirror Lake (10,040 feet, 6 acres) is a long, narrow lake sitting at the western end of the grassy meadow. A large rock outcropping lies along the northern shore, providing a scenic spot to grab a bite to eat or jump into the lake. Because of the sloped shores and the proximity of the trail to the lake, good campsites are nonexistent. Mirror Lake offers fair fishing for small cutthroat trout.

To continue to Lake Margaret, follow the trail as it passes along

Looking east over Lake Margaret toward the Continental Divide.

the northern shore of Mirror Lake. About ½-mile beyond Mirror Lake, the trail rises above the northern end of Lake Margaret, which is visible below. One-quarter mile beyond where Lake Margaret first becomes visible, the trail forks (**Point C**). Take the left fork (#1168A), which leads south to Lake Margaret and the other lakes in this area. (The right fork leads to Swamp Park.) Trail #1168A continues through the trees along the northern shore of Lake Margaret, dropping down to the north shore of the lake approximately ⅓-mile from the fork.

Lake Margaret (9,987 feet, 29 acres) is the largest lake in this chain. It is forested on all shores, but most areas consist of a narrow band of trees in front of rocky outcrops that drop down to the lakeshore. The Continental Divide is visible beyond the eastern shore of the lake. There are ample sites for camping on all sides of Lake Margaret, and good fishing for cutthroat, rainbow, and brook trout to sixteen inches.

From the western shore of Lake Margaret, continue west toward Lake Edward. Only ⅒-mile beyond the western edge of Lake Margaret the trail reaches the eastern edge of Lake Edward (**Point D**). Continue along the northern shore of Lake Edward until you reach the northwest corner.

Lake Edward (9,867 feet, 15 acres) is a large lake with a long "finger" extending along its northern shore to the west. A meadow surrounds the far western shore. Good campsites are concentrated along the northeast shore. Open shorelines provide good opportunities to fly-fish for plump ten- to thirteen-inch cutthroat trout.

From the northwest corner of Lake Edward, head south through a small meadow and over a small knoll before descending steeply to Snowstorm Lake (**Point E**), $\frac{1}{4}$-mile beyond Lake Edward. Snowstorm Lake (9,747 feet, 8 acres) has trees near all its shores except the north, where the trail reaches the lake. However, the trees are set back several hundred feet from the water, making Snowstorm Lake another ideal spot for fly-fishing enthusiasts. As in the other lakes in this chain, lily pads cover the shallow areas. Snowstorm Lake sits in a depression, rather than a basin, so the surrounding slopes are gentle and good campsites abound. The lake is brimming with small brook trout.

The trail continues along the northwestern shore of Snowstorm Lake, arriving at Fishhawk Lake (**Point F**) (9,700 feet, 10 acres) within $\frac{1}{10}$-mile. The shoreline surrounding Fishhawk Lake is flat, grassy, and swampy; better campsites are available at Snowstorm Lake. Small brook and cutthroat trout abound in Fishhawk Lake, and the open shoreline allows for unobstructed casting.

Mount Ethel

Trailhead
> *Wyoming Trail (#1101) at Buffalo Pass*

Starting elevation
> *10,300 feet*

Ending elevation
> *11,924 feet*

Distance (round trip)
> *19 miles*

Time required (round trip)
> *9.5 hours*

Rating
> *Moderate*

Maps
> *7.5' Buffalo Pass*
> *7.5' Mount Ethel*
> *Routt National Forest*

Main attractions .
> *Spectacular views from large, flat summit; easy access from the Wyoming Trail.*

Mount Ethel is most conspicuous when approached from the east, particularly while hiking up the Rainbow Lakes Trail (#1130). Its massive, snowclad, sheer eastern flank gives the impression that Mount Ethel's summit is attainable only by experienced mountaineers. However, the forbidding precipices on the east face hide the gentle and inviting incline that leads to the large level summit from the west. In fact, the top of Mount Ethel is so unassuming when viewed from the west that many hikers on the Wyoming Trail (#1101) stroll past without taking advantage of the breathtaking views atop its summit, a scant ½-mile to the west. Its easy access and unsurpassed views make a trip to the summit of Mount Ethel a must for hikers in the central Mount Zirkel Wilderness.

Mount Ethel is a long day hike from the Wyoming Trail trailhead at Buffalo Pass (**Point A**). We recommend Mount Ethel as a day-hike destination from a base camp in the interior of the Mount

Although the views from the summit of Mount Ethel are spectacular in every direction, the view of Slide and Rainbow lakes is particularly impressive.

Zirkel Wilderness (e.g., Luna Lake, Lake of the Crags, Roxy Ann Lake, Slide Lakes).

Follow the directions to Buffalo Pass on page 107. From the trailhead, follow the Wyoming Trail (#1101) north for 7 miles to the Lake Elbert/Luna Lake turnoff. Further description of this route is given in the Luna Lake, Lake Elbert hike narration on page 117. About 200 yards before reaching the turnoff to Lake Elbert (which is marked by a sign), the Wyoming Trail forks very faintly to the right (**Point B**) and continues north along the Continental Divide. Two rock cairns on the ridge to the north mark the point where the Wyoming Trail passes over the hill. If you reach the sign for Lake Elbert and Luna Lake, backtrack and look for the turnoff for the Wyoming Trail at Point B.

Continue to follow the Wyoming Trail as it meanders above timberline. The trail fades in a few areas, but careful observers can usually spot a cairn to point out the route. The views of Luna Lake from the Continental Divide are outstanding. Two miles past Point B the trail intersects the Crags Trail (#1182) (**Point C**). The summit of

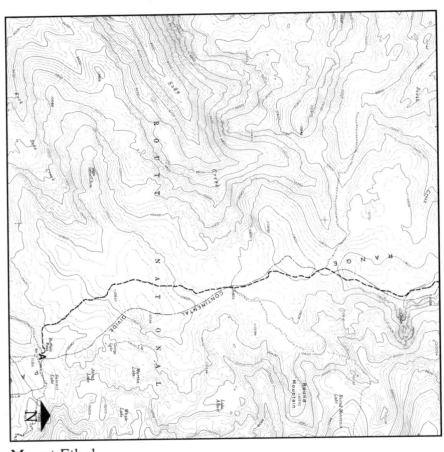

Mount Ethel

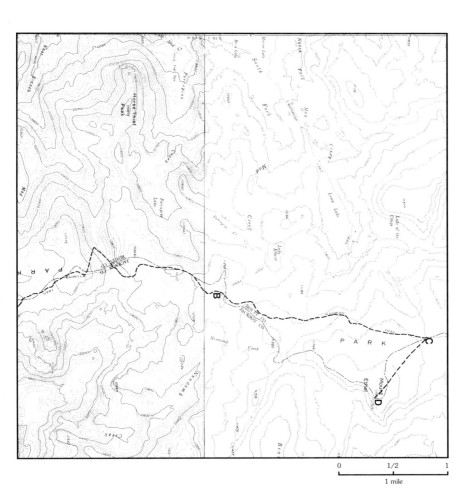

Mount Ethel lies ½-mile to the southeast (to your right and behind you). Leave the Wyoming Trail here and head southeast.

There is no defined route to the summit; simply aim for the highest point. The slope leading to the summit is very gentle. As you near the top, the views to the north become increasingly spectacular as Mount Zirkel, Red Dirt Pass, and the Sawtooth Range all come into view. The entire summit area is relatively flat with numerous lichen-covered rocks and a few large rock outcroppings. The true summit of Mount Ethel (**Point D**) is not readily distinguishable. The best views are from the rock outcrops along the sheer northeast face of the mountain and look down the valley containing Slide and Rainbow lakes. Use caution near the edges of the summit—the dropoffs are precipitous. The summit is a good spot to see ptarmigan, medium-size birds that spend most of their lives in the tundra above timberline. Ptarmigan are masters of camouflage, their mottled-brown summer plumage turning white to match the first snows of winter. After you enjoy the incredible vistas in all directions, rejoin the Wyoming Trail for the return trip.

Lost Ranger Peak

Trailhead
>   *Wyoming Trail (#1101) at Buffalo Pass*

Starting elevation
>   *10,300 feet*

Ending elevation
>   *11,932 feet*

Distance (round trip)
>   *20 miles*

Time required (round trip)
>   *10 hours*

Rating
>   *Moderate/Difficult*

Maps
>   *7.5' Pitchpine Mountain*
>   *7.5' Mount Ethel*
>   *Routt National Forest*

Main attractions
>   *Easy climb to summit from Wyoming Trail; spectacular
>   views from the heart of the Wilderness; summit register
>   to record successful ascents.*

As the Wyoming Trail (#1101) meanders along the Continental Divide, it passes through rugged scenery well above timberline. The highest point near the trail is atop Lost Ranger Peak, which, at 11,932 feet, affords a commanding view from the heart of the Wilderness. Lost Ranger Peak is accessible from all directions but difficult to reach in a single day. The route described is from the south along the Wyoming Trail, which involves a slightly longer hike than the route from the west. However, the southern route involves less elevation gain and offers outstanding views along the Continental Divide throughout the hike. Realistically, any attempt to scale Lost Ranger Peak should be planned as a day hike from a base camp near the middle of the Wilderness Area (e.g., Luna Lake, Lake of the Crags, North Lake, Wolverine Lakes Basin, or Roxy Ann Lake).

Follow the directions to Buffalo Pass on page 107. From the

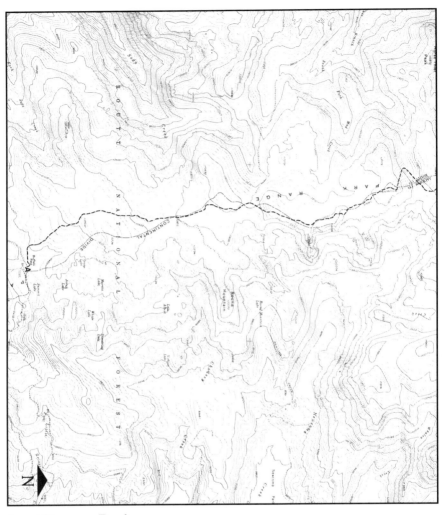

Lost Ranger Peak

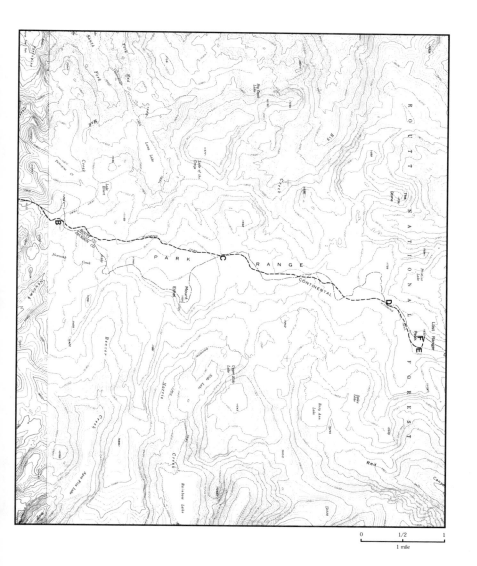

*The view to the north from the summit of Lost Ranger Peak. The summit
cairn is in the right foreground.*

Wyoming Trail trailhead (**Point A**) follow the directions to Lake
Elbert/Luna Lake on page 117. About 200 yards before reaching
the turnoff to Lake Elbert (which is marked by a sign), the Wyoming
Trail forks very faintly to the right (**Point B**) and continues north
along the Continental Divide. Two rock cairns on the ridge to the
north mark the point where the Wyoming Trail passes over the hill.
If you reach the sign for Lake Elbert and Luna Lake, backtrack and
look for the turnoff for the Wyoming Trail at Point B.

Continue to follow the Wyoming Trail as it meanders above
timberline. The trail fades in a few areas, but careful observers can
usually spot a cairn designating the route. The views of Luna Lake
from the Continental Divide are particularly striking. Two miles past
Point B the trail intersects the Crags Trail (#1182) (**Point C**).
Continue north on the Wyoming Trail. This section of the trail is not
well defined, but rock cairns guide the way. The Dome (to the left)
and Lost Ranger Peak (to the right) dominate the view to the north.
The few trees that survive at this altitude grow low to the ground in
tight clusters, their branches growing opposite the direction of the
prevailing winter winds. About 1 mile past the Crags Trail intersection,

Roxy Ann Lake is visible far down to the right (east). Bypass the turnoff to Roxy Ann, Slide, and Rainbow lakes and continue to a low saddle (**Point D**) just below Lost Ranger Peak. Continue along the Wyoming Trail as it heads uphill to the right, following a series of cairns through alpine tundra and scattered clumps of windblown trees. About ½-mile past the saddle, the trees to the left disappear and the slope leading to the summit becomes more gradual (**Point E**). At this point turn left (west) and aim for the highest point above the trail. The summit of Lost Ranger Peak is only $\frac{1}{10}$-mile west of the Wyoming Trail.

The summit of Lost Ranger Peak (**Point F**) is rolling and flat. Numerous lichen-encrusted boulders lie on the tundra. The summit is marked by a large rock cairn, which hides a register for all who climb the peak. The views in all directions are outstanding: virtually the entire Mount Zirkel Wilderness unfolds around you. To the north, Mount Zirkel, Big and Little Agnes mountains, and the Sawtooth Range are clearly visible. Northwest from the summit, Ptarmigan and Wolverine lakes glisten in the valley below. The Dome commands the western skyline, and Mount Ethel rules the southern panorama.

Lost Ranger Peak is also accessible from the eastern and western edges of the Mount Zirkel Wilderness. From the east, begin at the Grizzly-Helena Trail (#1126), 1 mile north of Red Canyon Reservoir. The rough road to the trailhead requires a high-clearance vehicle. Follow the Grizzly-Helena Trail south 1 mile to an intersection with the Lost Ranger Trail (#1131). The Lost Ranger Trail climbs steadily 7 miles to an intersection with the Wyoming Trail, 1.5 miles north of Lost Ranger Peak.

The North Lake Trail (#1164) is the access route from the west. Follow the North Lake Trail as it ascends 5 miles to meet the Wyoming Trail at the Continental Divide. The Wyoming Trail leads south 3 miles to Lost Ranger Peak.

The Dome

Trailhead
> *Wyoming Trail (#1101) at Buffalo Pass*

Starting elevation
> *10,300 feet*

Ending elevation
> *11,739 feet*

Distance (round trip)
> *24 miles*

Time required (round trip)
> *14 hours*

Rating
> *Very Difficult*

Maps
> *7.5′ Buffalo Pass*
> *7.5′ Mount Ethel*
> *Routt National Forest*

Main attraction
> *Breathtaking views from atop the most distinctive peak in the Wilderness Area.*

In the central portion of the Mount Zirkel Wilderness, one's attention is inevitably drawn to the distinctive silhouette of "the Dome." From the Wyoming Trail (#1101) near Mount Ethel, the Dome dominates the view northward and lures adventurous hikers to ponder the views from its rocky crown. As is true of the other destinations in the central portion of the Mount Zirkel Wilderness, the Dome is accessible from all directions. However, distance and difficulty dictate that the hike to the top of the Dome cannot be accomplished from any trailhead in a single day. This hike is intended as a strenuous day hike from a backcountry camp in the interior of the Wilderness (e.g., Wolverine Basin Lakes, Luna Lake, Roxy Ann Lake). The route described is from the intersection of the Rainbow Lakes Trail (#1130) and the Wyoming Trail (#1101) (**Point A**).

From Point A, leave the Wyoming Trail and angle northwest over a small saddle toward the Dome. There is no trail, but the

The route to the summit of the Dome is the most challenging hike in this guide. The best approach involves scrambling to the flat area left of the Dome before ascending the ridge to the summit.

route is above timberline with the Dome remaining clearly in view. Continue through a grassy meadow and a collection of small ponds lying in a depression (**Point B**). From this low spot, head for the high point on the rocky ridge south of the Dome. Continue walking toward the Dome while staying high on the ridge. The ridge ends at a large boulder field (**Point C**), beyond which lies the forbidding southern face of the Dome. Before entering the boulder field, take several minutes to plan your best route to the summit. We recommend scrambling across the large, angular boulders to the point at the base of the Dome where the vegetation descends to the lowest level. Carefully ascend the very steep, loose rock (scree) slope to a level forested ridge below the left (west) side of the summit. Be sure to climb this scree slope one hiker at a time, or two hikers side by side, because each hiker will dislodge rocks and send them hurtling down the slope (which is very dangerous to hikers below). From the forested ridge, follow a game trail east along the ridgeline as it climbs steeply several hundred feet to the summit. Be cautious of the exposed dropoff to your right.

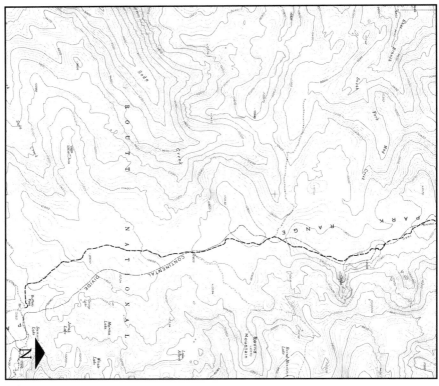

The Dome

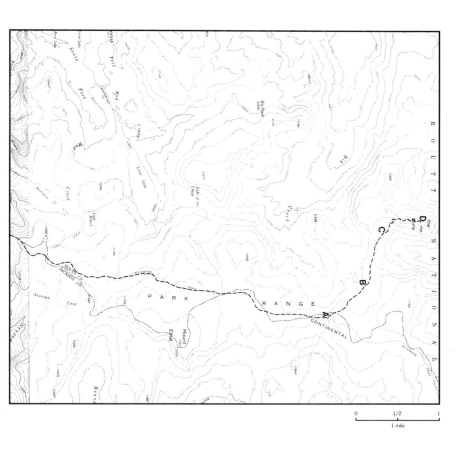

0   1/2   1

1 mile

The summit of the Dome (**Point D**) is surprisingly flat and grassy. The views in all directions are immense. Less than 2 miles to the east, Lost Ranger Peak dominates the skyline. Mount Ethel juts up along the Continental Divide to the south. To the north, Red Dirt Pass, Mount Zirkel, and the Sawtooth Range are easily discerned. Far to the northwest, the distinctive, lightly colored crown of Hahn's Peak can be seen. Dome Lake shimmers in its basin 1,700 feet below the north edge of the summit.

Return to the Wyoming Trail via the same route, using extreme caution when descending the scree slope above the boulder field. Since the route to the Dome is very demanding and seldom-traveled, we recommend this hike be attempted by experienced hikers only, in groups of two or more.

Destinations in the Surrounding Routt National Forest

Although the main focus of this book is hiking in the Mount Zirkel Wilderness, we have included several short hikes in the Routt National Forest, which surrounds the Wilderness. Most of the routes described in this section are short hikes to scenic lakes featuring good fishing. Lake Dinosaur, Long Lake, and Lost Lake are the most popular destinations. Also included is a description of the route to the distinctive twin-spired summit of Rabbit Ears Peak, which dominates the skyline from the east side of Rabbit Ears Pass.

The hikes in this section can be completed in a half-day or less, and most are ideal for families. Since these trails are outside the Wilderness boundary, they are also open to mountain bikes, which are not allowed in the Wilderness.

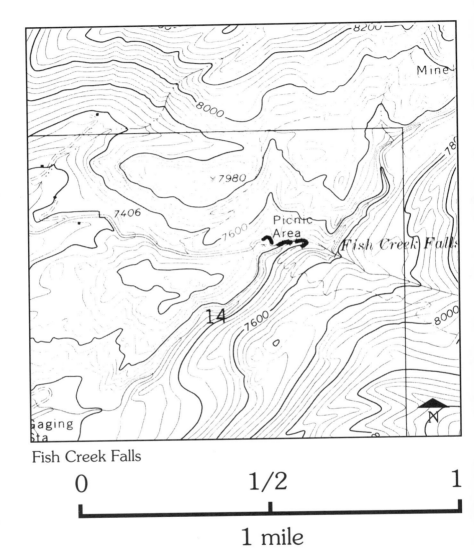

8200

Mine

8000

780

×7980

7406

Picnic
Area

7600

Fish Creek Falls

14

7600

8000

N

Gaging
Sta

Fish Creek Falls

0   1/2   1

1 mile

Fish Creek Falls

Trailhead
> *Fish Creek Falls Trailhead (#1102)*

Starting elevation
> *7,650 feet*

Ending elevation
> *7,550 feet*

Distance (round trip)
> *1/2-mile*

Time required (round trip)
> *30 minutes*

Rating
> *Easy*

Maps
> *7.5' Steamboat Springs*
> *Routt National Forest*

Main attractions
> *An easy walk to a large waterfall; picnic area.*

Fish Creek Falls is a popular destination for vacationers and Steamboat Springs locals alike. The short hike can be combined with a picnic lunch to create an enjoyable outing. The falls are an impressive 289 feet high and only a short walk from the parking area.

To reach Fish Creek Falls, turn right (west) off of Highway 40 onto Third Street in downtown Steamboat Springs. Immediately turn right onto Oak Street. Follow Oak Street until it becomes an all-weather dirt road called Fish Creek Falls Road. After 2.9 miles, Fish Creek Falls Road enters the Routt National Forest Recreation Area. Just over 3 miles from downtown Steamboat Springs, the road ends at the Fish Creek Falls parking area.

Two short trails to the falls leave from the parking area. One trail leads to a viewing area above the waterfall. The second leads to the base of Fish Creek Falls and the Long Lake picnic area. Both hikes are easy 1/4-mile walks. Those who wish to hike farther can continue on the Fish Creek Falls Trail (#1102) past the base of the waterfall, and eventually arrive at Long Lake, 4.5 miles to the east.

A short walk leads to the base of Fish Creek Falls.

Hinman Lake

Trailhead
> *Hinman Lake Trailhead*

Starting elevation
> *7,718 feet*

Ending elevation
> *8,195 feet*

Distance (round trip)
> *4 miles*

Time required (round trip)
> *2 hours*

Rating
> *Easy*

Maps
> *7.5' Farwell Mountain*
> *Routt National Forest*

Main attractions
> *Short hike to mountain lake; easy road access; can be shortened to 2 miles round trip for families with young children.*

The trail to Hinman Lake passes through abundant aspen and open meadows before arriving at the small mountain lake. Vegetation surrounding the lake is a study in contrasts—aspen and wildflowers border two sides of the lake, spruce and fir ring the rest. The hike to Hinman Lake is a 4-mile round trip, but the distance can be halved for families with young children (and a four-wheel-drive vehicle).

To reach the trailhead, take Routt County 129 north from Steamboat Springs for 17.4 miles to Forest Service Road 400 (Seedhouse Road). Forest Service Road 400 is an all-weather dirt road that does not require four-wheel-drive. Follow Forest Service Road 400 for 5.4 miles to Forest Service Road 430. (*Note:* There is a turnoff to the Hinman Campground approximately ½-mile before Road 430. Hinman Campground is not the trailhead for Hinman Lake.) There is no sign marking the Hinman Lake trailhead; simply

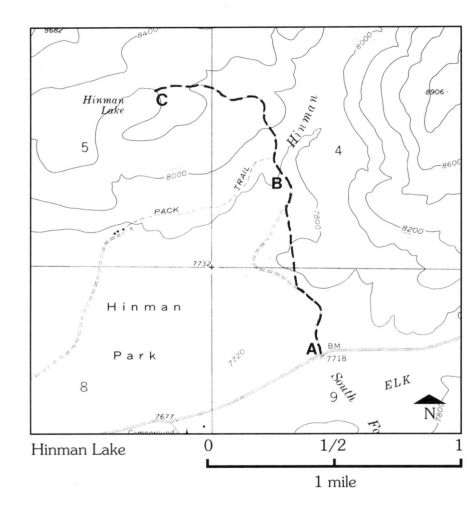

Hinman Lake

0 1/2 1

1 mile

Aspen lining the trail to Hinman Lake.

park near the intersection and proceed up Road 430 on foot. If you are in a four-wheel-drive vehicle and wish to shorten this hike, it is possible to follow Road 430 approximately 1 mile to Hinman Creek, where you must park and continue to the lake on foot.

From the intersection of Road 400 and Road 430 (**Point A**), follow Road 430 north and east around a lush aspen forest. While hiking to Hinman Lake, we have seen many deer and other animals in the abundant vegetation that lines the trail. About ⅛-mile from the trailhead there is another logging road off to the left; stay on the main road. One-quarter mile from the trailhead, the road turns and heads north. It enters an older spruce/fir forest and branches again two more times before arriving at Hinman Creek. At each fork, stay to the right on the main road. As the road approaches Hinman Creek it skirts a large expanse of private land. Do not cross the fence delineating the private land off to the left (west).

Cross Hinman Creek (**Point B**) 1 mile from the trailhead and begin climbing the heavily vegetated embankment on the other side. After climbing the embankment, turn south and walk along a ridge for approximately ⅛-mile. The views from the ridge are of green hills and meadows speckled with the white bark of aspen. The trail forks shortly after rounding the southern portion of the ridge; take the right fork, which turns and heads north. At this point begin a ¾-mile, fairly steep climb through thriving aspen stands and lush vegetation. Stop and look for hummingbirds, bees, and other wildlife among the wildflowers and grasses. The final climb to the top of the hill consists of a short series of switchbacks. Be sure to take in the beautiful views to the southeast from this vantage point. After crossing through an open meadow and reentering the aspen, stay to the left where the trail forks as it emerges from the aspen. Within 50 feet the trail forks again; stay to the left and follow the trail another 100 feet to Hinman Lake (**Point C**).

Hinman Lake (8,195 feet, 4 acres) is a shallow spring-fed lake that does not support a fish population. With the exception of the south side, the rim around the lake is marshy and covered with lily pads and cattails. The north and east shores of the lake are lined with aspen and wildflowers, and the south and west sides are exclusively fir and spruce trees. All sides of the lake are fairly hilly and steep and not suitable for camping. The trail circles the lake and is a worthwhile walk, but it does not lead to any other destinations.

Rabbit Ears Peak

Trailhead
Rabbit Ears Trailhead
Starting elevation
9,740 feet
Ending elevation
10,654 feet
Distance (round trip)
2.5 miles
Time required (round trip)
1.5 hours
Rating
Easy/Moderate
Maps
7.5' Rabbit Ears
Routt National Forest
Main attractions
Short walk to summit of a distinctive peak; fine views from summit.

With twin volcanic spires jutting from its summit, Rabbit Ears Peak is aptly named and easy to spot from the east side of Rabbit Ears Pass. Although it appears quite rugged from afar, a well-defined trail leads right to the base of the "ears." The trail is short but fairly steep and provides an ideal family outing. Rabbit Ears Peak is the highest point in the area, affording unsurpassed views in all directions.

To reach the trailhead, take Highway 40 to Dumont Lake Campground near Rabbit Ears Pass. Follow the main road toward Dumont Campground. Drive past the picnic area and campground to a turnoff on the left (1.5 miles from Highway 40). Turn left at the Rabbit Ears monument; a sign indicates Forest Service Road 311 straight ahead. When dry, Road 311 is passable with a two-wheel-drive vehicle, but four-wheel-drive is recommended. Follow Road 311 for ¼-mile to a post on the right side of the road marking Forest Service Road 291. Road 291 is very rough and requires four-wheel-drive.

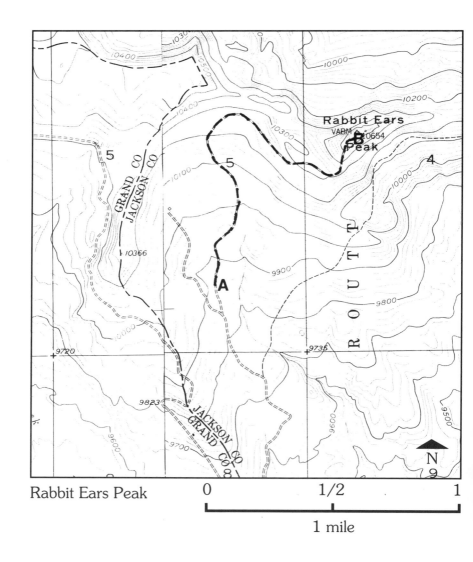

Rabbit Ears Peak

0   1/2   1

1 mile

Looking north to Rabbit Ears Peak from Highway 40.

The trail to Rabbit Ears Peak is actually a continuation of Road 291. We recommend parking just before Road 291 crosses a stream (**Point A**), 1.2 miles from the intersection of Road 311 and Road 291, and hiking the rest of the way to the summit.

One-third mile from the trailhead, enter an open area teeming with wildflowers. At this point Rabbit Ears Peak disappears from view behind the trees off to the right. One-half mile farther, stop and enjoy the views behind you down the valley to the south. Head up a fairly steep hill, which crests ¾-mile from the trailhead. There is an old road to the left of the trail at the top of the hill; continue following the main road to the right as it meanders along the ridge through abundant wildflowers. At mile 1.1 the road becomes a trail and begins its final, steep ascent to the summit. Two-tenths of a mile later the trail ends at the base of the "ears" (**Point B**).

Admire the geology of Rabbit Ears Peak, but be sure to stay on the path that leads around the base of both ears. The Rabbit Ears are composed of very crumbly volcanic rock and should not be climbed on. Spectacular views from the summit of Rabbit Ears Peak include the Mount Zirkel Wilderness to the north, the Medicine Bow National Forest farther north beyond the Zirkels, the Rawah Wilderness to the east, and the Flattop Range far to the south.

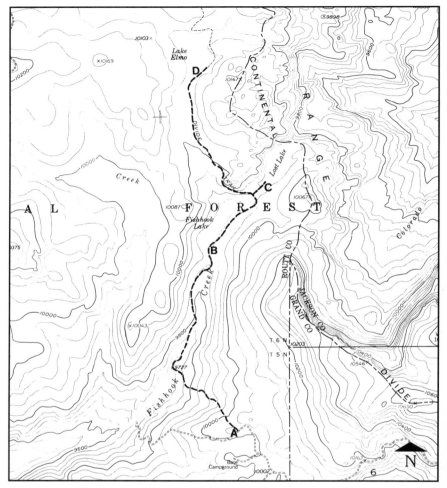

Fishhook Lake, Lost Lake, Lake Elmo

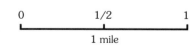

0   1/2   1

1 mile

Fishhook Lake, Lost Lake, Lake Elmo

Trailhead

Base Camp Trailhead (#1102)

Starting elevation

10,000 feet

Ending elevation

Fishhook Lake: 9,877 feet
Lost Lake: 9,900 feet
Lake Elmo: 10,038 feet

Distance (round trip)

Fishhook Lake: 3 miles
Lost Lake: 4 miles
Lake Elmo: 6 miles

Time required (round trip)

Fishhook Lake: 1.5 hours
Lost Lake: 2 hours
Lake Elmo: 3 hours

Rating

Easy/Moderate

Maps

7.5' Mount Warner
Routt National Forest

Main attractions

*Opportunity to explore and fish at three different lakes
in a half-day; little elevation gain.*

Fishhook Lake, Lost Lake, and Lake Elmo are scenic high-country lakes lying in close proximity to one another in the Routt National Forest south of the Mount Zirkel Wilderness. The trailhead is only a short drive from the developed Dumont Lakes Campground just off Highway 40 near Rabbit Ears Pass. These fairly short, level hikes are ideal for those seeking a quick backcountry escape. All three lakes offer good fishing, so pack a fishing rod and bring back a few trout for a campsite cookout.

To reach the Base Camp trailhead, take Highway 40 to Dumont Lake Campground near Rabbit Ears Pass. Follow the main

Fishhook Lake.

road toward Dumont Campground. Drive past the picnic area and campground to a turnoff on the left (1.5 miles from Highway 40). Turn left at the Rabbit Ears monument and follow the sign to Forest Service Road 311. When dry, Road 311 is passable with a two-wheel-drive vehicle, but four-wheel-drive is recommended. Beautiful wildflowers and outstanding panoramic vistas embellish the 4.3-mile drive on Road 311 to the trailhead. At 4.3 miles, be alert for the trailhead sign on the right side of the road, because Road 311 continues past the trailhead. There are several good campsites available near the trailhead.

The Base Camp trailhead (**Point A**) is the southern terminus of the Wyoming Trail (#1102/1101), which extends north to the Wyoming border. The trail begins as a wide, well-defined path that immediately winds downhill through spruce and fir. Just over ½-mile from the trailhead the trail levels out in a wet meadow covered with false hellebore (cornhusk lily) and willow. Two-tenths of a mile later, drop into a valley alongside Fishhook Creek for a short distance, then cross the creek. One-half mile later the trail reaches Fishhook Lake (**Point B**).

Fishhook Lake (9,877 feet, 10 acres) is a long shallow lake

View of Lost Lake from its rocky western shore.

surrounded on all sides by spruce and fir. Along the northern shore of the lake, willow, grasses, and boulders predominate as the spruce and fir thin out. The northwest side of Fishhook Lake is the most heavily vegetated, with trees growing within ten feet of the water's edge. Fishhook Lake offers fair fishing for small brook trout.

To continue to Lost Lake and Lake Elmo, follow the trail around the east side of Fishhook Lake. After crossing Fishhook Creek, the trail enters a campsite. At this point the main trail divides into two trails. The trail to the left, below the campsite, is a swampy fisherman's trail that skirts the lakeshore and leads to the northern shore of the lake. For those not planning to fish, we recommend following the main trail, which stays 200 to 300 feet above the swampy area. The main trail veers slightly uphill and cuts through the campsite; it can be picked up as it heads right (east) just behind the large boulder above the campsite. This trail reaches the northernmost tip of Fishhook Lake ³⁄₁₀-mile later, then continues north through a grass meadow before entering the forest. About ½-mile beyond Fishhook Lake the trail forks; take the right fork, which leads in ¹⁄₁₀-mile to Lost Lake (**Point C**).

Lost Lake (9,900 feet, 20 acres) is larger, deeper, and more picturesque than Fishhook Lake. A large rocky slope dominates the western shore of the lake and offers beautiful views from its summit. Lost Lake is surrounded on all sides by mature spruce and fir. Campsites are difficult to find here; the only established campsite we know of is to the right of the trail as it arrives at the lake. Fishing at Lost Lake can be excellent for brook and rainbow trout to twelve inches.

To continue to Lake Elmo, hike back to the trail intersection just west of Lost Lake and follow Trail #1102 north. Lake Elmo (**Point D**) is approximately 1 mile beyond the intersection. Lake Elmo (10,038 feet, 13 acres) lies at the headwaters of Fishhook Creek and offers good fishing for brook trout to twelve inches.

Grizzly Lake

Trailhead
>Wyoming Trail (#1101) on Forest Service Road 310
>(Divide Road)

Starting elevation
>10,500 feet

Ending elevation
>10,202 feet

Distance (round trip)
>3 miles

Time required (round trip)
>1.5 hours

Rating
>Easy

Maps
>7.5' Buffalo Pass
>Routt National Forest

Main attractions
>Level, short walk along the Continental Divide ending at
>a scenic lake; good family hike.

The route to Grizzly Lake follows the Wyoming Trail, which hugs the Continental Divide for 47 miles from the Base Camp trailhead to the Wyoming border. The trail to Grizzly Lake passes through both forest and meadow, bypassing many small lakes and ponds along the route. This hike is an ideal outing for families with young children.

The trailhead to Grizzly Lake is located on Forest Service Road 310 near Buffalo Pass. Follow the directions to Buffalo Pass on page 107. At the summit of Buffalo Pass, Road 60 intersects Forest Service Road 310. Turn south onto Road 310 and follow it for 1.6 miles. The sign marking the trail to Grizzly Lake is on the left side of the road, just after you drive under the power lines. The trailhead marker for Grizzly Lake (**Point A**) reads "Wyoming Trail #1101/Base Camp Trailhead."

The trail immediately turns right, heading south and paralleling Road 310. The first of a series of white posts marking the trail

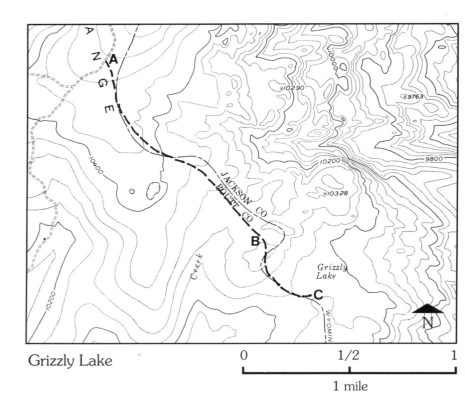

Grizzly Lake

0   1/2   1

1 mile

A short hike along the Wyoming Trail leads to Grizzly Lake.

appears just ⅛-mile into the hike. Just over ¼-mile from the trailhead, the trail fades somewhat in a marshy area and becomes difficult to follow. By walking straight across the marshy area and veering slightly to the right toward the trees, you can relocate the trail. One-half mile from the trailhead, wind through a sparsely forested area with a small pond visible to the right. Just under 1 mile a small lake can be seen through the trees off to the left (**Point B**). This is not Grizzly Lake. Continue on past two more large ponds on the right and cross a small stream.

One mile from the trailhead, enter a large meadow. The trail cuts across the width of a meadow, continuing east. A cairn marks where the trail reenters the forest after crossing the meadow. One and a half miles from the trailhead, pass through a small clearing and look for Grizzly Lake, which is visible through the trees off to the left. Leave the main trail and walk several hundred feet to the southern shore of Grizzly Lake (**Point C**).

Grizzly Lake (10,202 feet, 4 acres) is surrounded on all sides by wet, grassy meadows. Mature spruce and fir circle the meadows 100 to 150 yards from the lake. Grizzly Lake is shallow and does not support a fish population.

We recommend Grizzly Lake as a day hike only; plenty of campsites are available at nearby Summit Campground and Granite Campground. The Wyoming Trail continues south from Grizzly Lake, intersecting the trail to Round and Percy lakes after 2.5 miles.

Lake Dinosaur

Trailhead
> *Lake Dinosaur Trailhead on Forest Service Road 310 (Divide Road)*

Starting elevation
> *10,087 feet*

Ending elevation
> *10,182 feet*

Distance (round trip)
> *2 miles*

Time required (round trip)
> *1 hour*

Rating
> *Easy*

Maps
> *7.5' Buffalo Pass*
> *Routt National Forest*

Main attractions
> *Easy hike to a pristine spring-fed lake; good fishing for six- to ten-inch brook trout.*

The short walk to Lake Dinosaur rewards hikers with good fishing at a scenic backcountry lake. The trail is not well defined in spots and following it can be tricky, but with the help of our directions and the knowledge that the lake lies below a hill visible from the trailhead, we are confident that anyone who wants to visit Lake Dinosaur can readily do so.

The trailhead for Lake Dinosaur is located on Forest Service Road 310 near Buffalo Pass. Follow the directions to Buffalo Pass on page 107. Two hundred feet beyond the Wyoming Trail trailhead at the summit of Buffalo Pass, Road 60 intersects Forest Service Road 310. Turn south onto Road 310 and follow it for 3.4 miles to the Lake Dinosaur trailhead (**Point A**). There is no sign marking the Lake Dinosaur trailhead, but several clues will help you find it: 1. there is a small turnout on the right side of the road 3.4 miles from the intersection of Roads 60 and 310; 2. the turnout is just past a

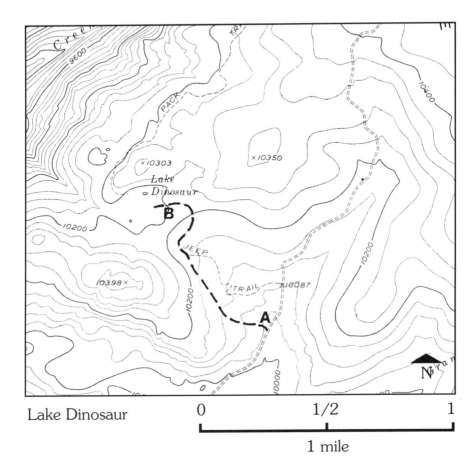

Lake Dinosaur

0   1/2   1

1 mile

The spring-fed waters of Lake Dinosaur.

small waterfall on the right and a culvert under Road 310; and 3. a rocky hill lies on the right side of the road at the turnout. Park in the turnout.

As you face west, the trail to Lake Dinosaur begins between the small waterfall on your right and the rocky hill on your left. For the first ⅓-mile the trail is distinct as it heads west through a large grassy meadow. The trail disappears in a marshy area about 100 feet below the base of the hill on the west side of the meadow. There is a post marking the route through the marshy section. To relocate the trail, head right (north), skirting the trees at the base of the hill on your left. Hike approximately ⅓-mile to the north side of the hill. Look for an opening in the trees to your left, on the north side of the hill just above the area where the hill becomes flat and opens into another meadow. At this point turn left (west) and walk along the left edge of the opening. The trail reappears as a well-defined old road near a large rock on your left. The trail remains distinct from this point on and leads ⅓-mile to Lake Dinosaur (**Point B**).

Lake Dinosaur (10,182 feet, 9 acres) is surrounded by spruce and fir trees. A large rock outcrop along the west shore provides prime fishing spots for six- to ten-inch brook trout. Lake Dinosaur is a popular camping destination; fire rings and good campsites can be found along the east and west shores. Take time to follow the trail to the southern end of the lake to see the springs that feed Lake Dinosaur. These springs are surrounded by wildflowers well into August each year and provide a beautiful backdrop for photographs.

Long Lake, Round Lake, Lake Percy

Trailhead
> *End of Forest Service Road 310 near Granite Campground at Fish Creek Reservoir*

Starting elevation
> *9,900 feet*

Ending elevation
> *Long Lake: 9,880 feet*
> *Round Lake: 10,060 feet*
> *Lake Percy: 10,035 feet*

Distance (round trip)
> *Long Lake: 3 miles*
> *Round Lake: 5 miles*
> *Lake Percy: 5.2 miles*

Time required (round trip)
> *Long Lake: 1.5 hours*
> *Round Lake and Lake Percy: 2.5 hours*

Rating
> *Easy*

Maps
> *7.5' Mount Werner*
> *Routt National Forest*

Main attractions
> *Short, level hike to a chain of mountain lakes; good fishing for pan-size brook trout.*

The hike to Long Lake, Round Lake, and Lake Percy is ideal for those who desire a quick backcountry getaway. These lakes offer some of the best camping and fishing opportunities in the Routt National Forest. Long Lake, Round Lake, and Lake Percy can be reached by trail from all directions. From the east, Forest Service Trail #1134 leaves Hidden Lake Road (Forest Service Road 40) 2.5 miles south of Hidden Lake Campground and climbs steeply (gaining 1,035 feet in elevation in 2 miles) as it passes Lake Percy and Round Lake on its way to Long Lake. Forest Service Trail #1102 from the Base Camp trailhead winds 5 miles to Long Lake from the

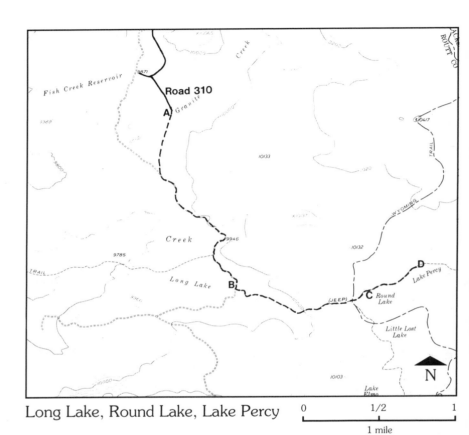

Long Lake, Round Lake, Lake Percy

Despite its popularity, forty-acre Long Lake never feels crowded.

south, passing Round Lake en route. Access from the west is approximately 4.5 miles to Long Lake via Forest Service Trail #1102, which leaves from the parking lot of Fish Creek Falls just east of Steamboat Springs. The route described below is the hike from the north, which involves the most difficult road access but is the easiest hiking route to all three lakes.

The trailhead is located at the end of Forest Service Road 310, near Buffalo Pass. Follow the directions to Buffalo Pass on page 107. At the summit of Buffalo Pass, turn south onto Road 310 (toward Fish Creek Reservoir) and follow it 5 miles until it ends just south of the turnoff to Granite Campground at Fish Creek Reservoir. The trailhead is on the left side of the road, where it dead-ends (**Point A**). Plenty of campsites are available at nearby Granite Campground.

The trail to Long Lake (#1102) is marked by a brown plastic post. The trail is well defined as it heads gently uphill through spruce and fir. About ½-mile from the trailhead the trail intersects an old road. Turn left and follow the road downhill. The remainder of the route to Long Lake follows this wide road, which is closed to motorized vehicles but popular with mountain bike enthusiasts.

Therese and Kootenai relax along the shore of Lake Percy.

(Mountain bikes are permitted on trails in the Routt National Forest, but not on trails in the Mount Zirkel Wilderness.) At mile 1.2 the road intersects a second road; stay left to continue to Long Lake. Immediately beyond this intersection Long Lake becomes visible through the trees. The trail circles down to the east end of the lake **(Point B)**.

Long Lake (9,880 feet, 40 acres) is indeed a long, narrow lake with an island near its western shore. Due to its accessibility from all directions, the lake is a very popular destination. Fortunately, its large size provides plenty of solitude for those who seek it. The northern and western shores are mostly forested, but some open stretches along the north shore provide good spots to fish for brook trout to twelve inches. Plenty of campsites are available on all sides of the lake.

To continue to Round Lake and Lake Percy, pick up the trail on the eastern shore of Long Lake where it turns left (east) at an old signpost. This well-defined turnoff is located 100 feet north of the inlet stream. Just over ¾-mile from Long Lake, cross a large open meadow and begin winding uphill into spruce and fir. One mile beyond Long Lake the trail reaches a four-way intersection.

At the intersection, continue straight on Trail #1134 to Percy Lake. Only ¼-mile past this intersection the trail reaches the northwestern shore of Round Lake (**Point C**).

Round Lake (10,060 feet, 16 acres) sits in a shallow depression and is surrounded by relatively level shoreline. Spruce and fir reach down to the water's edge on all sides of the lake, and lily pads extend into the shallow western section of the lake. Good campsites are scattered in the trees around the lake. Round Lake offers good fishing for small brook trout.

To continue to Lake Percy, follow the trail along the northern shore of Round Lake to its eastern edge. Lake Percy (**Point D**) is just over the hill to the east, ¹⁄₁₀-mile from Round Lake.

Lake Percy (10,035 feet, 17 acres) is larger and longer than Round Lake. Lily pads cover its western and northern shores, with deeper water along the eastern bank. Fishing for Lake Percy's plentiful brook trout is most successful along the deeper eastern shore. Good campsites are on the northern and southern sides. We found many fire rings situated too close to the lake; be sure to choose a campsite at least 100 feet from both shoreline and trail.

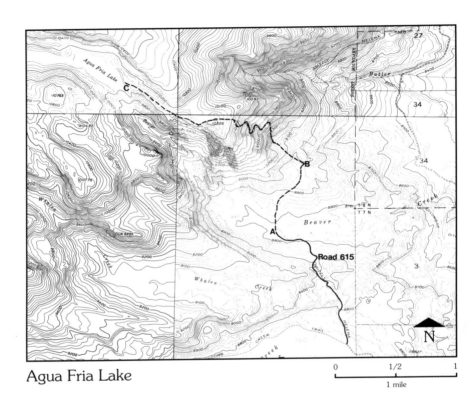

Agua Fria Lake

Agua Fria Lake

Trailhead

Grizzly-Helena Trailhead (#1126) on Forest Service Road 615

Starting elevation

8,800 feet

Ending elevation

10,040 feet

Distance (round trip)

6 miles

Time required (round trip)

3 hours

Rating

Moderate

Maps

7.5' Teal Lake

7.5' Buffalo Pass

7.5' Pitchpine Mountain

7.5' Mount Ethel

Routt National Forest

Main attractions

Beautiful views down the Beaver Creek valley.

Agua Fria Lake is actually a reservoir formed by a dam on Beaver Creek. The lake itself is not particularly scenic; the high point of this hike is the beautiful views as the trail climbs above the low-lying areas to the east. Since most of the trail follows an old four-wheel-drive road that is outside the Mount Zirkel Wilderness, it receives some use from dirt bikes, all-terrain vehicles, and mountain bikes. Be sure to bring plenty of water (and sunscreen) on warm sunny days because the majority of this hike is out in the open.

To reach the trailhead, take Highway 14 west out of Walden to Hebron. Turn right (west) at Hebron and continue on Jackson County Road 24 for 11.2 miles until you reach the Grizzly Campground. Drive just past the campground and turn right onto Forest Service Road 615. Follow Road 615 for 5.6 miles until it dead-ends

Distant views to the east from the Agua Fria Trail.

at the Grizzly-Helena Trail (#1126) (**Point A**). The sign at the trail-head indicates Rainbow Lakes, Red Canyon, and Lone Pine Road.

The Grizzly-Helena Trail immediately crosses Beaver Creek and enters a lodgepole pine forest with unusually large numbers of dead and downed trees. About 1 mile from the trailhead the old road leading to Agua Fria Lake intersects the Grizzly-Helena Trail to your right (east) (**Point B**). Continue straight at the intersection, following the old road for the remainder of the hike. One-half mile farther, climb through a sparse aspen forest with beautiful views looking out over the lowlands to the east. The trail eventually levels out and begins to head gradually downhill above Beaver Creek and Beaver Creek Canyon. The trail reaches Agua Fria Lake (**Point C**) 3 miles from the trailhead.

Agua Fria Lake (10,040 feet, 28 acres) is surrounded by brown rocky slopes, with snowy peaks rising beyond its western shore. The rocks above the eastern side of the reservoir afford impressive views and photo opportunities of the Beaver Creek valley. As in most reservoirs, the water level in Agua Fria Lake fluctuates during the year. In early summer the reservoir fills as the snow melts from the surrounding peaks. As summer progresses more and more water is released, and the reservoir water level drops. Due to the fluctuating water levels, the lake is not nearly as pretty as the natural lakes in the vicinity. Agua Fria Lake offers fair fishing for small brook trout.

Appendix: Fishing Destination Table

Lake	Elevation (feet)	Size (acres)	Maximum depth (feet)	Trout species present
Agua Fria Lake	10,040	27.6	59	Brook
Bear Lake, Lower	10,320	15.8	58	Cutthroat, Brown
Bear Lake, Upper	10,343	10.1	37	Cutthroat
Beaver Lake	10,340	7.0	20	Brook
Big Creek Lake	10,620	7.7	41	Cutthroat
Big Creek Lakes, Lower	8,997	350.7	57	Brook, Rainbow
Big Creek Lakes, Upper	9,009	101.2	30	Brown
Bighorn Lake	10,106	13.8	59	Cutthroat
Blue Lake	9,815	21.4	132	Lake, Brook, Rainbow
Ceanothuse Lake	9,560	10.0	29	Cutthroat, Rainbow
Crags, Lake of the	10,850	5.8	11	Cutthroat
Diana, Lake	10,268	9.1	16	Cutthroat
Dinosaur, Lake	10,182	9.4	27	Brook
Dome Lake	10,060	10.6	12	Cutthroat
Edward, Lake	9,867	14.8	45	Cutthroat
Elbert, Lake	10,800	11.0	35	Cutthroat, Rainbow
Elmo, Lake	10,038	12.6	8	Brook
Fishhawk Lake	9,700	7.4	24	Brook, Cutthroat
Fishhook Lake	9,877	9.5	5	Brook
Gem Lake	10,160	6.9	26	Brook
Gilpin Lake	10,338	28.9	60	Brook
Gold Creek Lake	9,555	8.2	34	Brook
Grizzly Lake	10,202	4.3	5	(no trout)
Hinman Lake	8,195	4.0	8	(no trout)
Katherine, Lake	9,859	23.0	115	Lake, Brook
Long Lake	9,880	40.0	32	Brook
Lost Lake	9,900	15.0	34	Brook, Rainbow
Luna Lake	10,482	38.2	55	Cutthroat
Manzanares Lake	9,238	4.2	13	Brook
Margaret, Lake	9,987	29.2	50	Cutthroat, Brook, Rainbow
Mica Lake	10,428	6.1	11	Brook, Rainbow
Mirror Lake	10,040	5.7	20	Cutthroat
North Lake	10,313	5.5	9	Brook
Peggy, Lake	11,165	9.8	31	Brook
Percy, Lake	10,035	17.0	23	Brook
Porcupine Lake	10,480	4.2	17	(no trout)
Pristine Lake	11,040	9.7	55	Brook
Ptarmigan Lake	10,699	7.3	16	Cutthroat
Rainbow Lake	9,854	96.0	91	Rainbow, Cutthroat
Rainbow Lake, Lower	9,700	9.0	29	Rainbow, Cutthroat
Rainbow Lake, Middle	9,830	9.0	33	Rainbow, Cutthroat
Round Lake	10,060	16.0	40	Brook

Lake	Elevation (feet)	Size (acres)	Maximum depth (feet)	Trout species present
Round Mountain Lake	9,860	10.0	11	Brook
Roxy Ann Lake	10,204	63.0	126	Cutthroat
Seven Lakes	10,773	14.0	25	Cutthroat
Slide Lake, Lower	10,527	27.2	65	Cutthroat, Brook
Slide Lake, Upper	10,760	8.6	35	Brook, Cutthroat
Snowstorm Lake	9,747	8.3	45	Brook
Three Island Lake	9,878	23.2	40	Brook
Twin Lake, Lower	9,865	23.0	39	Lake, Brook
Twin Lake, Upper	9,865	4.3	21	Brook
West Fork Lake	9,305	13.0	20	Brook
Wolverine Lake	10,284	7.0	25	Cutthroat

Index